ENGLISH CATHEDRALS
a personal pilgrimage

by

Edward Mayor

✺

For Frances Brealey

A Petwood Publication 2011

First Published, 2011

Copyright © The Petwood Hotel, Woodhall Spa, Lincolnshire

ISBN: 978-0-9561852-6-6

Cover Photos

Centre:

Norwich Cathedral
COURTESY OF NORWICH CATHEDRAL

Clockwise from top centre:

St. Paul's Cathedral
COURTESY OF ST PAUL'S CATHEDRAL

Bristol Cathedral
WITH THANKS TO THE CHAPTER OF BRISTOL CATHEDRAL

Lincoln Cathedral
COURTESY OF JOHN BYFORD

Winchester Cathedral
PHOTO BY JOE LOW, REPRODUCED BY KIND PERMISSION OF THE CHAPTER OF WINCHESTER

Exeter Cathedral
COURTESY OF THE DEAN AND CHAPTER OF EXETER CATHEDRAL COPYRIGHT ANGELO HORNAK

Canterbury Cathedral
COURTESY OF CANTERBURY CATHEDRAL

Printed by Cupit Print, The Ropewalk, Horncastle, Lincolnshire LN9 5ED

This Book belongs to

Address:

Telephone:

Email:

Down the Nave at St. Paul's Cathedral
COURTESY OF ST. PAUL'S CATHEDRAL

CONTENTS

Acknowledgments

I have enjoyed many conversations with people in all 28 of the medieval cathedrals, and several of the more modern cathedrals, and I am deeply grateful to them all for their help with images or information. Alphabetically by cathedral these are:

Bath: Andrew Desmond and Dr. Lucy Rutherford.
Blackburn: Pauline Rowe
Bristol: Sarah Morris
Canterbury: Jocelyn Prebble and Emma Clarke
Carlisle: Carolyne Baines and David Weston
Chelmsford: Rosie Baxter
Chester: Nick Fry
Chichester: Ruth Poyner and Maria Gordon
Derby: Irene Minton
Durham: Diane McIlroy
Ely: Lesley Anne Thompson
Exeter: Amanda Martin
Gloucester: Bairbre Lloyd
Guildford: Gill Thorpe and Paul Williamson
Hereford: Dominic Harver
Leicester: Richard Paterson
Lichfield: Claire Lamplugh and Chris Grey
Lincoln: Julie Wright

London St. Paul's: Anna Talbot
Norwich: Alan Kefford and Cecile Tuddenham
Oxford: Eileen Head and John Briggs
Peterborough: Sarah McGhee
Ripon: Ian Forster, Lt. Col. Ian Horsford and Gail Squires
Rochester: Dr. Edwina Bell, Deborah Macgee and Col. John Nowers (retd.)
Salisbury: Sarah Flannagan and Hannah Paye
Southwark: David Payne
Southwell: Caroline Jarvis
St. Alban's: Judith Card, David Kelsall and Hayley Lewis
Wells: Ruth Clacee-Rowe and Paul Richards
Westminster Abbey: Christine Reynolds
Winchester: Charlotte Barneville
Worcester: Sue Macleod and Chris Guy
York: Peter Young

My grateful thanks go to Reg Brealey for inviting me to undertake this project and for all his support and enthusiasm, Emma Brealey for her patient typing of the entire text and for the intelligence and enthusiasm which she has brought to the task, Andrew and Steve Newton at Cupits Printers of Horncastle, who as always, have risen to the challenge and designed a beautiful product, and, finally, my partner Jonathan Perks for supplying many contact details and enabling the months of writing to go as smoothly as possible.

INTRODUCTION

A cathedral is a church which contains the throne, or cathedra, of a bishop. It is often said today that the English are losing their national identity, but you only have to walk inside any of our medieval Anglican cathedrals to realise that these "worlds apart" are steeped in Englishness.

They remind us that the English prefer to encounter the Divine in nature, and preferably in the English hedgerow, as the carved leaves of Southwell and so many other cathedrals prove. Some cathedrals even resemble forests, and Exeter is a supreme example. The English love linear qualities, in art, music and architecture, and line quickly takes over from massive volume as the Anglicisation of the Gothic Style matures over the centuries, from 1066 to 1520. The English are "uneasy on the heights" as John Harvey, the great architectural historian reminds us, and rather than building tall, they build long, inviting the pilgrim to go on journeys down vaulted tunnels and around many corners, but inevitably climaxing in some spectacular East Window or High Altar.

Most English kings, queens, heroes and great figures in the arts are buried or commemorated in our cathedrals, as are the saints who inspired their building and the powerful bishops who rebuilt them. Their Master Mason architects travelled Europe and Scandinavia, many working on several cathedrals, and introducing astonishing technical advances in vaulting or buttressing. Many thousands of foreign visitors come to England every year to "do" Westminster Abbey and tour those cathedrals which have acquired international reputations. Just as we visit other countries to see how their buildings reflect their identity, so tourists come here to experience our cathedrals as an obvious indicator of Englishness. Inevitably, they also see the finest of English craftsmanship.

USING THIS BOOK

Within an illustrated historical and architectural introduction to each cathedral, a blank page awaits your own comments on your visit. You can "collect" all 28 of the great medieval buildings which are, or in two cases were, cathedrals, and you can also record your visits to the four entirely modern cathedrals and those which began as Parish Churches. A Glossary of terms and a Further Reading List may help you to deepen your enjoyment of all 44 cathedrals.

Brief mention must be made of several medieval masterpieces which have never been cathedrals, but which should not be missed. Beverley Minster and King's College Chapel Cambridge, are magnificent. On a more monastic note there is Tewkesbury Abbey, and the majestic ruins of Tintern, Fountains and Rievaulx Abbeys.

It has been fashionable to decry the work of great Victorian restorers like the Gilbert Scotts, but here you will find their contributions celebrated, for a cathedral is the sum of additions from every era and a living organism.

Each of the 28 medieval cathedrals has been invited to contribute two images for the book thus giving the reader an idea of how they would like to be represented visually. I am deeply grateful to them. Working on this book has been a great joy and the culmination of a lifetime of study and countless visits. I hope it will become your companion and your keepsake, as you set out on your own pilgrimage to collect our English cathedrals.

Edward R. Mayor, Woodhall Spa

N.B. Dates in brackets after the names of Master Masons or Bishops normally refer to the period of their involvement with each cathedral.

The works of architectural writers mentioned in the text are listed in the Further Reading list on page 112.

Lincoln Cathedral west towers from the south east
COURTESY OF JOHN BYFOR

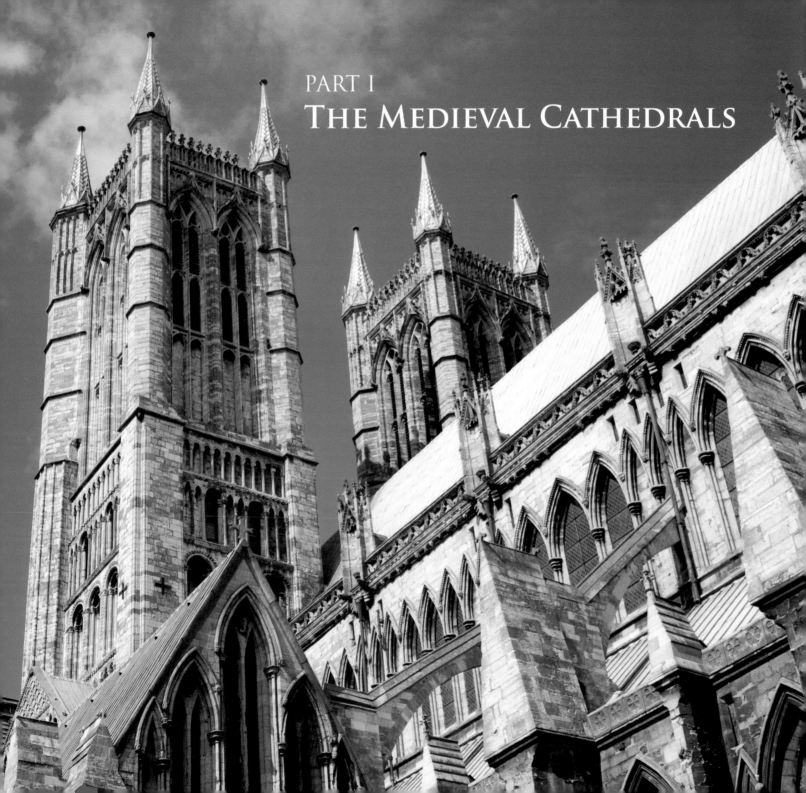

PART I
THE MEDIEVAL CATHEDRALS

BATH

Bath Abbey is included here, although it is no longer a cathedral, because of the magnificence of its interior which makes a small space seem much larger. This feeling is amplified once its great organ is played, and the vastnesses of a Louis Vierne symphony are resonating around its cliff-like columns. And yet this entire church takes up only the space of the nave of a former Norman abbey.

The present church of 1501-39, was built by Robert and William Vertue for Bishop Oliver King, and joins a select few cathedrals which for John Harvey "approach the ideal" as unified buildings. The prosperity of King Henry VII's time, reflected in his chapel at Westminster Abbey, is evident at Bath, and Robert Vertue worked on both.

According to John Harvey, the Vertues declared that "of the vault divised for the chancelle, there shall be noone so goodely neither in England nor in France". Bath's sumptuous vaulting becomes ever more intricate as it soars from the tall shafts into the fans, to swim at last in an ecstasy of tracery. Gone forever are the ridge ribs, even the lierne vaults of earlier times. The virtuosity of the Perpendicular style is here triumphant. It is hard to believe that we stand in a space only 225ft long and 75ft high. Sacheverell Sitwell concluded that the Bath vaults were palms rather than fans, "like a recurrent dream of Palm Sunday" and it is easy to agree with him.

The Perpendicular West Front at Bath Abbey
REPRODUCED WITH KIND PERMISSION OF BATH ABBEY

BATH *a personal pilgrimage*

There had been a Romanesque church on this site from c.1090-1120, but even before this, there had been a nunnery from 676. From c.970 to 1539, Benedictine monks ran an abbey.

In 1088, John de Villula prevailed upon King William II "Rufus" to make him Abbot of Bath and then its bishop, having removed the See from Wells in 1090. The See had been created at Wells in 909, so Villula's successor Bishop Robert of Lewes (1136-66) decreed that all bishops should be styled "of Bath and Wells", but in the end it took a Papal Resolution to make this binding in 1218. Bath Abbey was dissolved in 1539 leaving only the Chapter of Wells capable of electing a bishop and having a building in which his throne could be placed.

The city of Bath is a Georgian masterpiece, but there is no doubt that its abbey, with its glorious vaulting and virtual walls of light, is fully equal to its classical setting. From various vantage points, the elegant buttresses, Perpendicular tower with openwork parapets, and enormous clerestory windows beckon us in, irresistibly.

www.bathabbey.org

The Nave and Choir looking east, Bath Abbey
REPRODUCED WITH KIND PERMISSION OF BATH ABBEY

BRISTOL

Bristol Cathedral from the north east
WITH THANKS TO THE CHAPTER OF BRISTOL CATHEDRAL

Bristol Cathedral is a building of great beauty inside and out, with an elegant triple-towered profile and double-tiered tracery in its Decorated windows. Pevsner reserved his highest praise for Bristol which, he said, proves "that English design surpassed that of all other countries during the first third of the fourteenth century." And you can see the entire building shining in its bright stone across College Green with its distinctive staircase turrets on all three towers majestically capped with tall pinnacles. This amazing building has been playing second fiddle to Bristol's St. Mary Redcliffe church for far too long, and St. Mary's is, in many respects and as Queen Elizabeth I said, the "finest church" in her kingdom, but it is now time for the cathedral to take the stage.

The first establishment on the site was an Augustinian abbey founded by Robert Fitzharding, first Lord Berkeley, in 1140. Nothing of this abbey survives save the great Norman Chapter House, the undercroft of the refectory and a few bits of walling and arcading, but the chapter house features original interlaced blind arcading, of several types, and lozenge and zig-zag decoration. The huge vault ribs crackle with vitality. The chapter house has an international reputation.

There was no stopping Pevsner… "from the point of view of spatial imagination"…

the cathedral was "superior to anything else built in England, and indeed in Europe at the same time". Entering the nave, this spatial imagination is immediately apparent. Between 1868-88 George Edmund Street produced a nave which, after 350 years, completed work begun in the early sixteenth century. Street adopted the tierceron vault of Lincoln's nave for his five bays and the result is an optical heightening of the apex (also ridge-ribbed like Lincoln) despite the mere 52ft of its actual height.

But the exciting element in Bristol stems from this clever exploitation of the modest height, for in the north and south choir aisles, which are the same height as the nave and choir, the shaft mouldings on the pillars rise unbroken from floor to vault, while elegant cross arches brace the vault's thrust, and support unique lierne double vaults, set sideways. These are the tallest bay arches in England, rising to the full height of the vault,

and uniquely again, creating a Hall Church in which the aisles are as tall as the nave and choir, a feature very common in Germany, but only found in Bristol and in St. Michael's church, Bath, in medieval England. Abbot Knowle, between 1298 and his death in 1332, supervised this marvellous work.

The cathedral's two Lady Chapels contain many interesting items. The early thirteenth century Elder Lady Chapel was built by Abbot David who requested the Dean of Wells to send carvers to beautify the chapel, and the carvings resemble the famous capitals at Wells mentioned in the entry on Wells Cathedral. There are some exquisite animal carvings.

The Eastern Lady Chapel of c.1298 has glass showing the arms of Lord Berkeley and his relatives who fought at Crécy in 1346. The chapel has star-shaped niches with effigies of former abbots, while in the south choir aisle there is a unique double-star niche and further star niches along the wall.

King Edward II's sad story is encapsulated here in a north transept roof boss showing him naked except for his crown, while another shows him pointing to where he was murdered in 1327, at Berkeley Castle. These bosses are unique, but rivalling them in interest is a misericord in the choir of a man trying to whip a slug with a pack on its back! The Berkeley Chapel has the only medieval candelabrum in England, rescued from Bristol's Temple Church which was destroyed in the Second World War.

Finally, it was in Bristol Cathedral that the first women priests of the Church of England were ordained by Bishop Rogerson on March 12th, 1994.

www.bristol-cathedral.co.uk

The Nave and Choir of Bristol Cathedral showing the equal height of side aisles, nave and choir

WITH THANKS TO THE CHAPTER OF BRISTOL CATHEDRAL

CANTERBURY

To ethereal music, a young American soldier gazes in awe at the vault of Canterbury Cathedral. Outside, carved angels wait in silence for the climax of Powell and Pressburger's 1944 film *"A Canterbury Tale"*. In this classic portrayal of Englishness, Canterbury Cathedral becomes the main character. It begins with a flashback to Chaucer's Canterbury Pilgrims on their way to the greatest of all shrines in England, that of St. Thomas Becket, who was murdered in this cathedral as a result of the interpretation which several of King Henry II's knights placed upon his angry words about the powerful archbishop who dared to oppose him. The shrine no longer exists, but the Trinity Chapel and Becket's Crown, extending the Choir, are masterpieces of early English Gothic. There the saint's body was placed, to become the greatest goal of pilgrimage after Jerusalem and Rome.

St. Augustine came to Canterbury in 597 with forty Benedictine monks, and in the same year King Ethelbert was baptised there and enabled Augustine to establish a cathedral. Nothing remains of it now, but it was the last resting place of many great and scholarly men and archbishops. William the Conqueror dispossessed and imprisoned Stigand, the last of these Saxons, and appointed Lanfranc in 1070, three years after the cathedral had been destroyed by fire. Lanfranc rebuilt the cathedral and by 1093 when he died, there were over a hundred monks in his monastery of Christ Church. His successor, Anselm, died in 1109, but he had completed the great Norman crypt we see today. Building continued after 1175 under William of Sens, because of the murder and canonisation of Thomas Becket in December 1170 and 1173 respectively, which focused the attention of the whole of Europe on Canterbury.

French Master Mason William of Sens had watched the cathedral at Sens being built in the Gothic style, and after Canterbury Cathedral had been severely damaged by fire in 1174, he was engaged to rebuild it. From 1175 to 1180 he directed operations but a serious fall from a scaffold forced him to return to France. William the Englishman then took over and designed the Trinity Chapel and Becket's Crown, after completing his predecessor's work.

The only surviving twelfth century portrait of the saint is in the Becket window in the north aisle. The ancient thirteenth century glass of the eastern arm of the cathedral is exceptional and demonstrates that balance of colours with black and white which makes true medieval glass glow and sparkle at the same time.

For John Harvey, the nave is the supreme triumph of English architecture. It belongs to a golden age during King Richard II's reign in the 1390s, when Chaucer was Clerk of the

Canterbury Cathedral from the south west with its magnificent central 'Bell Harry' tower
COURTESY OF CANTERBURY CATHEDRAL

CANTERBURY *a personal pilgrimage*

DATE:

The Choir of Canterbury Cathedral with the Archbishop's Throne,
and beyond, the culminating space of 'Becket's Crown'
COURTESY OF CANTERBURY CATHEDRAL

Royal Works and Henry Yevele was his chief Mason and in his seventies. As though all previous attempts at bay design were but trials, here we experience an unhindered ascent to the vault, the shafts becoming lines of energy uninterrupted by the discreet shaft rings and capitals, and soaring into the fan vault. Tall aisle walls, occasioned by the cloisters to the north, lend the whole space a stately, yet understated, air. Add to this the beauty of the fan vault beneath the elegant central tower by John Wastell of 1493-97 and you have one of the best celebrations of Perpendicular architecture in England.

King Edward III's eldest son, Edward the Black Prince, who died in 1370, is buried here, as is King Henry IV. Since Henry VIII destroyed Becket's shrine, the tomb of the Black Prince has become a main goal of pilgrimage. The victor of the Battle of Poitiers in 1356, he was a great warrior.

The cloisters of 1397-1414, designed with lierne vaulting, and very open and light in feeling, have an impressive series of heraldic roof bosses. Henry Yevele designed the cloisters with Stephen Lote, who completed the upper parts of the Chapter House which had been built by Thomas of Canterbury, c.1304-20.

From well preserved twelfth century wall paintings and stunning thirteenth century glass to the four jewel-like south-east transept windows by Erwin Bossanyi in the twentieth, Canterbury Cathedral offers a rich feast of art and architecture. Prepared for the dramas to come through John Wastell's Christ Church Gate, we too can be pilgrims, in a Canterbury tale of our own.

www.canterbury-cathedral.org

CARLISLE

Carlisle Cathedral is a convincing demonstration of the way in which a severely truncated building can yet, with little more than its choir of eight bays, remain a magnificent space. Walking towards the south transept entrance, the situation becomes clear, for only two of the original eight bays of the nave are left. At the time of the Great Siege of Carlisle in 1644, one of the Civil War's most destructive episodes, six bays of the nave were demolished and carted off to provide fortifications.

The truncated nave is, however, of great interest. Very unusually, the piers of the central tower have their capitals halfway down. The Norman arches are distorted because mid-thirteenth century droughts caused resettlement in ground which had been disturbed by a changed water table.

In 685 St. Cuthbert came to Carlisle, and there are remains of a Saxon cross. The Danes sacked the town in 875. King William "Rufus" imposed English rule in 1092 because Carlisle was continually being fought over by the Scots and the English. He established a religious community here. King Henry I ordered Augustinian canons to take charge, creating the See of Carlisle in 1133. This automatically created a city, which would hopefully remain English, but which briefly returned to Scottish hands several times more. King Henry then made his father confessor, Adelulf, Prior of the Abbey and first Bishop of Carlisle. The canons continued at the abbey and cathedral until 1540.

The Romanesque nave and south transept of 1092-1123 was followed by the choir aisles and arcading between 1245-92, then by the choir piers and east bay, rebuilt after a fire in 1292, between 1293-1322, then the clerestory of the choir perhaps by John Lewyn, between 1363-95. The north transept, tower and choir stalls came later, between 1400-19.

The forty-six choir stalls are noted for their entertaining misericords. These include a man being swallowed by a dragon, a fox killing a goose, and a coronation of the Virgin. The well-known roof, painted in gold stars on a field of blue, was restored by 1970 and has remains of a hammer beam roof left at either side, though some authorities feel that the beams now decorated with angels are the sawn-off ends of tie-beams.

On the pier capitals of the arches around the choir you can find carvings of the Occupations of the Months – a medieval calendar in stone. January has the three-headed Janus looking back to the past, ahead to the present, and forward to the future.

Carlisle's finest architectural feature is the great East Window of 1245-92, a supreme

The East End of Carlisle Cathedral
COPYRIGHT© JAMES ARMSTRONG

example of the Decorated style and 51ft high. It may be the only nine-light window of the fourteenth century. Most of the glass dates from 1861 but the curvilinear tracery is original, and the finest in England.

The great restorer Ewan Christian (1814-95) was brought in by Bishop Tate and the building as we see it today is mainly the result of his work and that of Street, Blomfield, Charles Nicholson and Steven Dykes-Bower afterwards.

Carlisle's pulpit is from the little church in Cockayne Hatley in Bedfordshire. It had originally come from the church of St. Andrew in Antwerp and had been in Bedfordshire from 1826-1963. And in 1979 a beautiful Flemish altar piece called the Brougham Triptych was brought into the cathedral.

Carlisle may be the furthest north of our cathedrals, but it is well worth a leisured visit. It bears more scars than most, but it has one of the most beautiful Gothic spaces in England.

www.carlislecathedral.org.uk

Carlisle Cathedral ceiling and decorated 9-light window

CHESTER

If you want to savour the atmosphere of medieval monasteries before Henry VIII ruined them, you must go to Chester, where the cathedral is part of a superb monastery built between 1093 and 1530.

Sir John Betjeman penned deliciously comical poetry about the Victorian church restorers, and others have seen fit to pour scorn on their work, but all our great cathedrals have been altered continuously and restored after structural failure or siege. Most would not even be visitable had it not been for the likes of the Gilbert Scotts and the Blomfields, and this is so at Chester where the biggest restoration began in 1868 under Sir George Gilbert Scott, followed by the Blomfields, father and son. By 1818 it was on record that Chester Cathedral was in very poor shape with early restorations out of tune with its Gothic character.

The monastery buildings include a refectory with a stone pulpit built into the wall. While the Benedictine monks dined, one of them would read aloud from the pulpit. Originally, the monks had come from Abbot Anselm's former abbey of Beck in Normandy. Anselm became Archbishop of Canterbury and was canonised, but he came here to re-found an Abbey which in the early tenth century held the remains of St. Werburgh, the daughter of Wulfhere, King of Mercia.

Many people literally and metaphorically "see red" over the red sandstone of which the cathedral is built, but even Sacheverell Sitwell had to admit that despite the pervasive "unfortunate" sandstone, the choir stalls are

Chester Cathedral in the snow
COURTESY OF CHESTER CATHEDRAL

remarkable. Patrick Cormack, quite swept away, described them as "excitingly beautiful… perhaps the finest late fourteenth century wood carvings in Northern Europe". Of the forty-eight misericords beneath their elegant pinnacled canopies, some represent biblical scenes over three episodes, and there is a beautiful representation of Easter Morning, while the Dean's Stall has a Tree of Jesse and a figure in a wide-brimmed hat with a staff, "reminiscent of the charlatan or necromancer in paintings by Hieronymus Bosch" according to Sitwell, and identified as a pilgrim by Cormack.

In July 1541, the former Abbey of St. Werburgh became the cathedral of the new diocese of Chester. But apart from the choir stalls, all traces of the beauty of the cathedral were swept away in the Civil War, not least because of Chester's strong allegiance to the Crown. Despite a determined attempt at restoration by Bishop Stratford after the

CHESTER *a personal pilgrimage*

The Nave of Chester Cathedral looking east
COURTESY OF CHESTER CATHEDRAL

Restoration of King Charles II, nothing further was done, and the forlorn building was given the Sir George Gilbert Scott treatment from 1868-72. His work may divide opinion, but at least one window amongst all the Victorian glasswork stands out – A.W.N Pugin's "Resurrection". You can also find amongst the nineteenth century corbels, the heads of Gladstone and Disraeli!

Emulating the example at Chichester perhaps, Chester's Dean and Chapter ordered a free-standing bell tower, some fifty yards from the cathedral, to house the bells from the central tower. This was designed by George Pace and opened in 1975.

Regardless of its contentious restorations, Chester Cathedral makes a fine, almost dramatic ensemble in the busy city. Its monastic buildings and choir will make any visit memorable. And somewhere on the site is what Sitwell called "a perfect example of a slype". Exactly what and where this is, will be left for you to discover.

www.chestercathedral.com

CHICHESTER

All cathedrals are goals of pilgrimage, and Chichester is the last resting place of the remains of Gustav Holst (1874-1934) the most mystical of composers whose "Planets" suite is one of the summits of musical history. His ashes were interred here at the request of his friend the great Bishop George Bell (1929-58).

With its tall central spire of 277ft rebuilt from a design by George Gilbert Scott between 1861-66, it is the only English cathedral which can be seen from out at sea, apart from Portsmouth. While there is no sense, here, of a great Master Mason producing a rhythmical essay in living stone, Chichester has in its Retro choir perhaps the finest example of the Transitional style between Norman and Gothic. Here, the Purbeck marble shafts are attached and detached from the piers, and pointed arches span pairs of round ones. This was Bishop Seffrid II's finest achievement and he also introduced stone vaults and Purbeck marble shafting in the nave after a disastrous fire in 1187. His architect was probably Walter of Coventry.

Chichester's own saint, Richard of Wych, was bishop between 1245 and 1253, and like Thomas Becket or Hugh of Lincoln, he too had been critical of his King (Henry III) but he was renowned for his pastoral care. His shrine was destroyed and his bones scattered by Henry VIII's commissioners.

The effigy of Bishop Robert Sherbourne, Henry VII's Chancellor, is the finest in the cathedral. Beautifully restored, it is situated in the south wall, and the bishop is given one of the first true likenesses in the history of tomb sculpture.

Bishop Bell also has a lasting memorial in the form of the Arundel Screen. This great stone pulpitum across the nave had been removed by the Victorians just before the collapse of the spire in 1861. It was sensibly reinstated in 1960. Also in the 1960s, one of the most artistic deans in history, Dean Hussey, ensured that Chichester could boast items by several great contemporary artists. Thus we can enjoy the blazing red 1978 window by Marc Chagall (1887-1985) illustrating Psalm 150, the great psalm of praise, and a strikingly colourful tapestry by John Piper of 1966. There is a "Noli Me Tangere" by Graham Sutherland and a Cecil Collins altar frontal, "The Icon of Divine Light". Such pieces make up for the fact that Chichester has no medieval glass, thanks to vandalism during the English Civil War and the Commonwealth.

But the greatest items in the cathedral are amongst its oldest. Eric Gill and Henry Moore

The detached Bell Tower, West Towers and Spire of Chichester Cathedral
REPRODUCED WITH THE PERMISSION OF CHICHESTER CATHEDRAL

were both influenced by the two Romanesque relief carvings of the early twelfth century on the south wall, which show the Raising of Lazarus and Christ being greeted at Bethany by Mary and Martha. Their sculptor knew how the light could be made to assist in tense facial expression. They have survived for a thousand years to convey depths of piety and feeling which seem to derive from far older sculptural models – those of ancient Greek and Roman masks.

Chichester has the distinction of being the only English cathedral still to have an original detached bell tower, dating from the mid-fifteenth century. Standing to the north of the West Front, it was built by William Wynford (1360-1403) who also designed the cloisters. There is an intriguing "might have been", too, in that Christopher Wren was employed in rebuilding the spire during the reign of King Charles II, and was commissioned to rebuild the west end, but the plans were never carried out.

As one of William the Conqueror's first great cathedrals with a diocese founded in 1075, Chichester is a building of great age, in which masterpieces of twentieth century art shine out like jewels.

www.chichestercathedral.org.uk

Chichester Cathedral the Nave looking east
REPRODUCED WITH THE PERMISSION OF CHICHESTER CATHEDRAL

CHICHESTER *a personal pilgrimage*

DURHAM

Rising in a sublime cliff of warm brown stone from the gorge of the River Wear, Durham Cathedral from the railway is breathtaking. Often described as the finest English Romanesque cathedral, it is made vividly alive by the famous incised columns, unusual bay scheme, and fragrant atmosphere of this last resting place of St. Cuthbert and the Venerable Bede.

The carving of the incised columns and the dating of the nave's rib vault continue to cause international debate, a sure sign that we are dealing with a masterpiece. Were the columns carved in situ or pre-carved? Is the nave rib vault even earlier than the supposed earliest example at St. Etienne in Caen, or was it later?

The reader may consult the book list should they wish to enter the debate, but ultimately what matters is the quality of the architecture, and the spatial experience, and Durham has supreme quality.

There had been a monastery here from 993, where the relics of St. Cuthbert, Bishop of Lindisfarne, were kept. The building we see today was begun by Bishop William of St. Carileph in 1093, and continued by Ranulph de Flambard. The east section was completed by 1104 up to the second bay of the new nave, going westwards, and the relics of St. Cuthbert were brought in at that date. In about 1128 the cathedral was completed. Between 1242 and 1280, the Chapel of the Nine Altars was built at the east end by Master Richard of Farnham. Beneath the windows all around the inside are interlocking arches – the earliest

Durham Cathedral Nave looking west
COURTESY OF DURHAM CATHEDRAL & JARROLD PUBLISHING 2005

DURHAM *a personal pilgrimage*

in Britain. The nave vault has buttresses in the form of pointed arches, hidden in the galleries of the triforium. These arches are thought to have the earliest examples of flying buttresses in England, and the earliest pointed arches.

Durham's great incised piers demanded knowledge of complex geometrical procedures and each is a masterpiece of precision. Even the section through each pier was complex, because what seems to be a completely round pier becomes a columnar pier on the side facing the aisle.

Another masterpiece of precision which seems to suit its surroundings so well, is the 1380 Neville Screen of Caen stone behind the high altar. This was carved in London, perhaps by the great Henry Yevele, and brought to Durham by sea via Newcastle. It has lost its figures, and looks oddly contemporary, with a delicate and sustained effect.

Less delicate, but obligingly revealing of the splendours beyond, is Sir George Gilbert Scott's late nineteenth century Choir Screen, a triple-arched affair with its central one crowned by a gable which sweeps above the parapet. For Scott, it is a restrained work, and his pulpit rises to the side. Cormack tells us that no-one has had the courage to "tackle them", but why sweep away harmonious elements which tell a continuing story, just because they are Victorian?

Fronting the west end is the Galilee Chapel of c.1190, an unusual Romanesque space with slender piers and three tiers of double chevrons curving around the profiles of the arches. Perhaps the lovely atmosphere of the chapel derives from the presence of the tomb of the Venerable Bede (673-735), whose body was brought here in 1022 and laid in a tomb on the south side in c.1350. On the wall behind are Bede's words:

> *"Christ is the Morning star*
> *who, when the night of this world*
> *is passed*
> *Brings to His saints the promise of*
> *the Light of Life*
> *And opens everlasting day"*

Sir Walter Scott called Durham Cathedral "Half Church of God, half castle 'gainst the Scot", a concise summing-up but hardly doing justice to its beauty, which in part arises from the relationships between solids and spaces, and the filtration of light, and partly to the world-wide devotion of pilgrims through nine centuries.

www.durhamcathedral.co.uk

Choir and High Altar with the Neville Screen beyond
COURTESY OF DURHAM CATHEDRAL & JARROLD PUBLISHING 2005

ELY

As the train from Peterborough swings around Ely's southern slopes, the traveller sees a vision of stonework rising in so many stages that it appears to be climbing the hill. Ely Cathedral is a series of climaxes, each pinnacle and tower taller than the last. Our love of picturesque, irregular outlines and formations is something of a national characteristic, and is fully supplied by this tremendous "Ship of the Fens".

St. Etheldreda, Queen of Northumbria, founded a nunnery on the site in 673 but it was pillaged by the Danes in 869. Benedictine monks revived it in 970 and in 1081, Simeon,

a Norman Prior of Winchester became Abbot of Ely, and created a shrine to St. Etheldreda in his new Abbey Church, completed by 1189. The marshes around the Isle of Ely had sheltered one of the last pockets of Anglo-Saxon resistance to Norman rule. Hereward the Wake was their legendary hero but in the end the Abbey's monks helped the King to break him and his following. Today we stand in Simeon's original building except for the crossing and the choir. Ely had been elevated to cathedral status in 1109 when the Breton Abbot Hervé became the first bishop, the Pope having agreed to a new diocese made from part of the enormous diocese of Lincoln.

Entrance is gained via a later Galilee Porch projecting from the remaining two thirds of the original West Front, upon which many festive tiers of Romanesque arcades and roundels rise to a mighty west tower, and two smaller ones

closing the south side of the west transept. Ely has a lot of superb blind arcading of the late twelfth century, and this becomes even more lavish on the exterior of the nave and south aisles. The Prior's Door into the remains of the cloisters is internationally important as a wonderful example of detail overwhelming structure in English Romanesque work. The figures of the angels strenuously supporting Christ in His mandorla in the Tympanum over the door have toes reaching to the very edge of the lintel, while medallions of vine scrolls rush upwards into this tympanum, like ivy out of control.

Ely's great nave has three storeys in a 6:5:4 ratio. Almost certainly there would have been a barrel vault, but the immense "broken" wooden roof, richly painted, brings Ely's first great surprise, for it was executed during the Victorian restoration by a Mr. Le Strange of

BOTH PHOTOS COURTESY OF ELY CATHEDRAL IMAGE LIBRARY

*Ely Cathedral from the
meadow to the south*

*Ely Cathedral from the north-east,
showing the exterior of the vast Lady Chapel*

Hunstanton Hall and his friend Mr. Gambier Parry, without fee. But we are approaching the second and greatest surprise which has had enormous influence to this day.

Conductor and composer Leonard Bernstein got his wish to record Mahler's Resurrection Symphony here because of his admiration for the Octagon and Lantern, unique in Europe, and an engineering marvel.

When the central tower collapsed in 1322, Alan of Walsingham, then in charge of the building, conceived an octagonal crossing with a great star-shaped vault and lantern rising from eight pillars. John Ramsey and John Attgrene built the pillars but at almost seventy feet in span, the space proved beyond any mason's power to vault, so William of Hurley built it in wood. He found that the span went way beyond even the longest available timbers, so he created a hammer beam truss, which bore eight huge upright posts leading into the lantern. The roof of the lantern is another stellar vault. Those who sit down in this sublime space and gaze around will readily appreciate why the young Christopher Wren had been so impressed with the entire conception that his space beneath the dome of St. Paul's was inspired by Ely's Octagon.

While the enterprising Stained Glass Museum should not be missed, the Lady Chapel is our third great surprise and the largest in England, with the widest medieval vault. Beneath the windows is a riot of superb Decorated stone carving weaving in and out of each arcade with "nodding" ogee canopies curving forwards, upwards and sideways like flames. Add to these all the crocketting and statuary and you can see why Alec Clifton Taylor likened it all to a bed of parsley!

From Ely's lovely marina, up through the meadow by the cathedral with horses grazing, and up again to the festive turrets of a medieval romance, we see the sublime plan. Cathedral, city and endless fenland are suspended in a dream of England.

Website: www.elycathedral.org

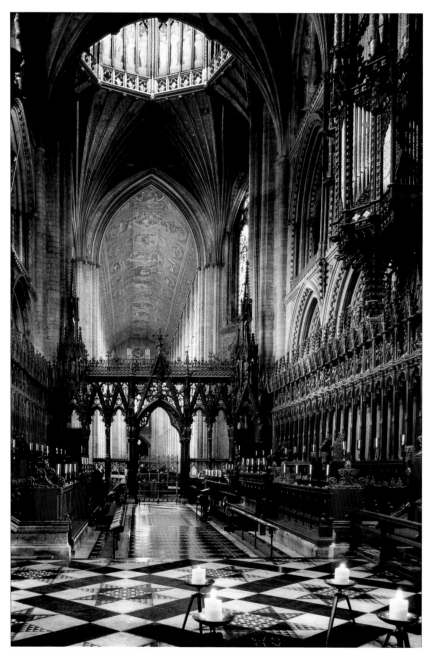

The Choir, Octagon, Lantern and Nave of Ely Cathedral

ELY *a personal pilgrimage*

DATE: _____

EXETER

The intimate relationship between Exeter and its cathedral is being enhanced at the time of writing by the creation of a new cathedral green with relaid paths, newly planted trees, and seats. This cathedral is a place of superlatives which will satisfy those in search of architectural unity.

The West Country See was transferred from Crediton to Exeter in 1049. Bishop Leofric was enthroned by Edward the Confessor as the first bishop of a new church which, on the evidence of its extant twin towers, must have been impressive. The towers rise above the north and south transepts to create an unusual ensemble more typical of Romanesque German churches.

The West Front (1328-75) is festive and comfortable. First, the stone screen by William Joy of 1329-46 exhibits three tiers of canopied saints and kings, several with legs eccentrically crossed and wearing richly folded garments. The Geometrical window behind the parapet of this screen has a lively rose of circled cinquefoils dancing with quatrefoils around a central five-lobed tracery. Some commentators find this West Front disappointing but the richness of its detail makes up for the lack of monumentality.

But there can be no reservations about Exeter's interior. It needs no guide book to tell us that this is the greatest Decorated interior in England, with richly moulded columns, arches, triforium and clerestory, topped by a vault of such energised ribs that it seems we are walking through a forest of soaring branches.

The north-west view of Exeter Cathedral showing one of the transept towers
COURTESY OF THE DEAN & CHAPTER OF EXETER CATHEDRAL   COPYRIGHT© ANGELO HORNAK

The dramatic perspective right down to the east window is in no way spoiled by the early fourteenth century screen bearing an organ which is thrilling to behold and thrilling to hear. The screen is alive with stonework which seems to ripple like flames.

The vaults rise to that quintessentially English feature, the ridge rib, which runs at the apex of the vault all the way down the building. The rib helps to heighten the vault because it appears to be a central beam coming from the east and rising as it comes towards us.

EXETER *a personal pilgrimage*

On the north side of the nave, an elegant minstrels' gallery interrupts the triforium, its purpose made clear by carved angels playing musical instruments. Today, choirs and ensembles use the gallery just as the medieval orchestras would have done. And at the springing point of each arch in the nave is an elaborate corbel carving, one showing an acrobat performing upside down over the head of a viol player, and others featuring the Green Man, who appears at least twenty times at Exeter.

Who is to thank for all this? John Harvey tells us that Thomas Witney (1316-42) masterminded the nave, and before him, Master Roger (d.1310) and William Luve (1310-16) built the rest apart from the Romanesque transepts and towers. The nave vault was by William Farleigh (1332-63). The man who probably inspired it all was Bishop Walter Bronescombe who died in 1280. He attended the consecration of Salisbury Cathedral in 1258. His tomb, gloriously restored, is alive with colour and gold.

There is one more bonus for visitors to Exeter Cathedral, for despite all its grandeur, it feels like home.

www.exeter-cathedral.org.uk

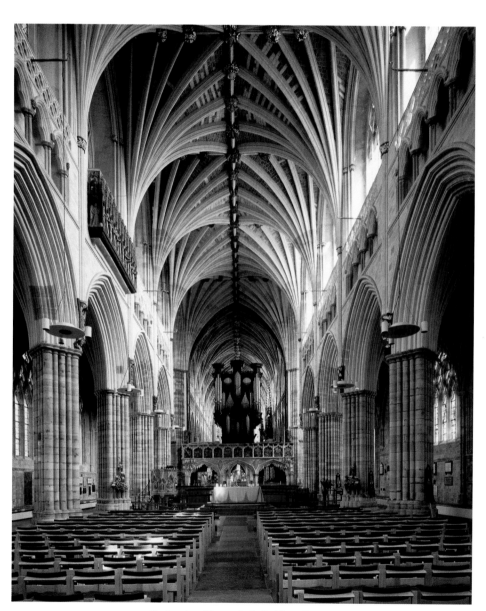

The interior of Exeter Cathedral from the west
COURTESY OF THE DEAN & CHAPTER OF EXETER CATHEDRAL   COPYRIGHT© ANGELO HORNAK

GLOUCESTER

Gloucester Cathedral is the text book demonstration of the enormous stylistic differences between the Romanesque and the Perpendicular. Outside, the superb Perpendicular central tower and west front of 1450-60, and the beautiful porch leads us to expect a similar interior, but we enter a massive perspective of exceptionally tall drum columns, devoid of all ornament save for a minimum around each bay. Osric, Prince of Mercia, founded the first monastery here in 681. After several destructions and rebuildings it became a Benedictine house. In 1048, William the Conqueror then appointed his chaplain Serlo to be the Abbot and by his death in 1104, one hundred monks were in residence. His great new abbey was dedicated in 1100 but out of this, only the crypt remains – a familiar tale. The stone vault of the next nave was apparently done by the monks and the lack of a Master Mason is evident, but the imposing dimensions of the space indicate the prominence and wealth of the Benedictines.

The Choir, one of the most dazzling in England, proves the pulling power of a brutally murdered monarch. King Edward II met a gruesome end at Berkeley Castle in 1327 at the

The South Porch of Gloucester Cathedral, gloriously restored
COURTESY OF GLOUCESTER CATHEDRAL

instigation of his Queen, Isabella, and her lover Roger Earl Mortimer. Brought by the Abbot himself to the cathedral, the King's body was solemnly buried here in the audacious presence of his murderers. His tomb became a shrine and he was venerated as a martyr.

With Gloucester suddenly a great centre of pilgrimage, the money poured in, and the result was the finest Perpendicular choir and biggest East Window in England, all expressed in soaring line and reaching a 92ft climax at the apex of the elaborate lierne vault, awash with gilded angels. The fourteenth century window, perhaps the gift of Lord Bradstone, whose arms it displays, has always been known as the Crécy Window on account of Bradstone and his friend Sir Maurice Berkeley fighting in that battle in 1346. There is a delightful subtlety too, for this enormous window is not one flat expanse, but like a medieval triptych, has angled side wings. In the glass itself, apostles, saints, abbots and bishops abound, and the principal subject is the Coronation of the Virgin.

King Edward II fared better in death than he ever did in life, for his tomb is a vision of the heavenly Jerusalem, its pierced and incised stonework culminating in a triumphant forest of pinnacles. Beneath, sunlight bathes his sensitive features on perhaps the finest of all alabaster Royal effigies.

The cloisters, finished around 1420, can claim to be the most beautiful in England, with the first large expanse of fan vaulting giving the sensation of stonework perpetually in motion. There are twenty recesses where the monks would work at desks, and a lavatorium, a long, lead-lined water trough where they washed. They have also featured in the blockbuster Harry Potter films, as the corridors of Hogwarts.

The central tower with its delicate openwork pinnacles and parapet and elegant diagonal buttressing, is amongst the most beautiful towers of the fifteenth century, vying for supremacy with that of Canterbury.

Completed at the end of the fifteenth century and also in the Perpendicular style, with its elegant bridge linking the north and south triforia, came the Lady Chapel, that extension of the east end which causes a dark shadow on the lower central portion of the Crécy window.

When King Henry VIII decided that Gloucester Cathedral would be the ideal new cathedral for a new diocese, he wrote that it was "a very fit and proper place...considering the site of the said late monastery in which many famous monuments of our renowned ancestors, Kings of England, are erected." It became the "Cathedral Church of the Holy and Undivided Trinity", and today it offers an object lesson in the ways that stone can be made into a gravity-denying medium, soaring to celestial heights.

www.gloucestercathedral.org.uk

The Fan-vaulted Cloisters of Gloucester Cathedral
COURTESY OF GLOUCESTER CATHEDRAL

GLOUCESTER *a personal pilgrimage*

HEREFORD

Many pilgrims come to Hereford Cathedral to encounter the medieval mind in the form of the famous Mappa Mundi and the chained library, but the cathedral itself offers a great deal to lovers of the Romanesque and devotees of the great Victorian restorers, the Scotts. Sir George Gilbert Scott and his brother John Oldrid were active here and George made a great screen, which was ripped out in 1967, an action now regretted by many.

Hereford Cathedral
FOTOLIA COPYRIGHT© JENNY THOMPSON

The See was established early, in 676, but there is no trace of the first cathedral which was dedicated to St. Ethelbert, King and Martyr. A church on the site burned down in 1054, and although repaired, was again destroyed to make way for the present building.

With its ample central tower, the cathedral looks very striking from across the River Wye and the beautiful countryside around, but the tower is an Early English design of 1325, while the West Front is an early twentieth century dream of Decorated Gothic by J. Oldrid Scott, with enormous pinnacles, castellated corner towers and massive buttresses protecting a beautiful central door with a trefoiled gable and a central "trumeau" post, backed by an imposing seven-light Geometrical window to the west end. This new west front was no whim, for a western tower had collapsed and destroyed the earlier front.

Hereford has links to two other cathedrals, Norwich and Lincoln. The builder of Norwich Cathedral, Herbert de Losinga, had a brother who as Bishop of Hereford was responsible for much of the present building. Soon after 1079, Robert de Losinga decided on a new cathedral for Hereford and his new eastern end was eventually consecrated in 1110, after which the nave and side aisles were added to the transepts in the usual manner.

The east wall of the southern transept is fascinating. The first central tower collapsed c.1110 and perhaps as a result of rebuilding, there is an altered gallery tier, which towards the tower suddenly has a much larger arcade. The variety of blind arcading and gallery openings on this wall creates a satisfying abstract experience, with a much later lierne vault rising unobtrusively from the slimmest of ribs.

Lincoln Cathedral has the link with the Mappa Mundi. Not only was it painted by Richard of Holdingham, Treasurer of Lincoln Cathedral, but it may also have been painted there, because of the prominence given to Lincoln on the map. It is thought that Richard, who was also a Prebendary of Hereford, painted it c.1275. He died c.1313. Jerusalem is at the centre of the map, while demon-freaks of

the medieval imagination abound.

Then we have the marvellous Chained Library, the largest of its kind to survive, and moved, with the Mappa Mundi, to a fine new building west of the cloister in 1996. Each of its 1500 handwritten and printed books has a chain attached to the front edge of one cover and to a rod on the bookcase. Only by turning a key to release a rod may a book be removed.

Hereford Cathedral was the setting for one of King Stephen's coronations. Already crowned in December 1135, he was crowned again in Hereford on the Feast of Pentecost in 1138. An ancient wooden chair in the Sanctuary is thought to have been his throne. Hereford's saint was much more interesting, for St. Thomas Cantilupe came to Hereford as its bishop in 1275 having already been Chancellor of the University of Oxford and briefly Chancellor of England. He died in Italy in 1282 but became a cult figure on account of his goodness and piety. His bones, returned to Hereford, became a magnet for flocks of pilgrims who reported miracles. He was canonised in 1320. So popular was his cult that as a result of money given to the cathedral, the central tower was rebuilt – in 1325.

John Harvey maintained that of the Gothicised cathedrals, only at Hereford do extensive remains of the Romanesque building exist, and some details could easily be overlooked, but deserve mention here – the wonderful capitals on the drum columns in the nave. In the rush to the Mappa Mundi, these capitals should not be missed!

www.herefordcathedral.org

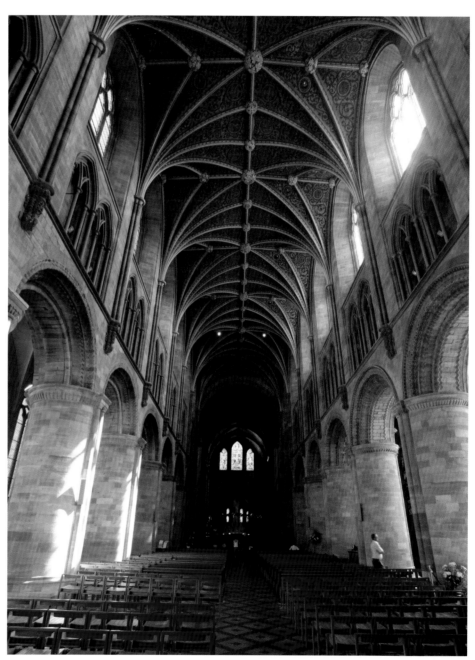

Hereford Cathedral
FOTOLIA COPYRIGHT© JENNY THOMPSON

LICHFIELD

"The most carved of all Decorated cathedrals, outside and in, is the stately Lichfield, with its three red sandstone spires."

So thought John Betjeman, and indeed those spires, nicknamed the Ladies of the Vale, rise in festive tiers, and feature pretty window openings, while the tall central gable of the West Front, the trefoils, quatrefoils and cinquefoils and the ranks of saints all add up to a sumptuous celebration.

The lower section of the West Front was probably by Thomas Wallace and the upper part by Nicholas of Eyton, all between 1265 and 1327. But the Victorian restorers have been heavily at work, and all but three of the statues are Victorian – indeed a figure of Queen Victoria herself joins them. However, the Scott family (Sir George and his brother John Oldrid) completely and sensitively restored the cathedral from 1856-1884, and Sir George's iron and brass pulpit and chancel screen are high water marks of Victorian design.

The interior is a glorious unity, with nave bays of exceptional beauty celebrating the very early Decorated style, with triple trefoils in the clerestory, quatrefoils in the triforium, and bisected cinquefoil mouldings in the spandrels of the main arcade. John Harvey names the masons at Lichfield as a family called Wallace – Thomas (c.1230-50), son William (c.1250-65) and one Thomas Wallace the Welshman

Lichfield Cathedral west front with the three 'Ladies of the Vale' Spires
COPYRIGHT© CLAIRE LAMPLUGH

(c.1265-80). The entire building took just under two hundred years to complete, between 1195 and 1385 when Gilbert Mason probably made the spires.

Lichfield sustained more damage in the English Civil War than any other great cathedral. The central spire was destroyed, the roof was smashed as a result, and the place used as a quarry. It took Bishop John Hacket some eight years from 1661 to see that the place was restored, and he gave a massive £1,683.12s to the fund.

Lichfield's Chapter House (c.1239-49), with its carvings almost equalling the excellence of those in Southwell's chapter house, contains other great treasures. In 1795, the cathedral was given some sixteenth century Flemish glass from the Abbey of Herckenrode near Liège after its dissolution. The French Revolution's cast-offs became one of Lichfield's glories. The eighth century illuminated Gospel of St. Chad is the cathedral's greatest treasure and one of the most beautiful examples of English Christian art. Chad was a great missionary who was Bishop of all Mercia from 669 to 672. His See was centred in Lichfield until William the Conqueror moved it to Chester, and it then moved to Coventry after 1095. Lichfield kept cathedral status, and there was a repeat of the Bath-Wells situation (see Bath Abbey) until 1836 when Coventry was dropped.

No traces of St. Chad's churches in Lichfield remain but in the first Norman church of Bishop Roger de Clinton, St. Chad's shrine became the centrepiece and the Saint's popularity led to the building of the present cathedral, with a Chapel of St. Chad's Head in the south transept.

Lincoln has its Imp, and Lichfield its Sleeping Sisters, a marble carving by Sir Francis Chantrey which caused a national sensation and is still a goal of pilgrimage today for all who have lost loved ones. The little Robinson girls died young and in 1812 their mother, the wife of Canon William Robinson, commissioned this tender realistic group of the daughters asleep in one another's arms, with snowdrops, upon a rolled mattress. But Lichfield has not forgotten two of its greatest sons, the lexiocographer Dr. Samuel Johnson and the finest actor of his day, David Garrick, whose busts can be found here.

The unity and beauty of Lichfield Cathedral is every bit as moving as Chantrey's masterpiece.

www.lichfield-cathedral.org

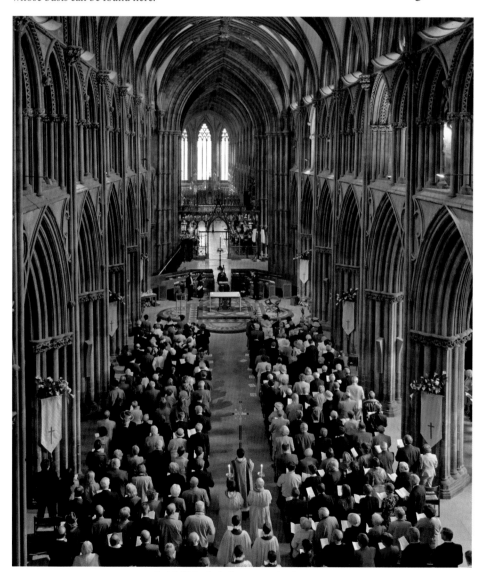

Lichfield Cathedral on Easter Sunday 2011
COURTESY OF LICHFIELD CATHEDRAL

LICHFIELD *a personal pilgrimage*

DATE: _____

LINCOLN

D. H. Lawrence loved Lincoln Cathedral and captured its power in his novel, The Rainbow in 1915:

"Here the stone leapt up from the plain of earth, leapt up in a manifold clustered desire each time, up, away from the horizontal earth…and there was no time nor life nor death, but only this, this timeless consummation, where the thrust from earth met the thrust from earth, and the arch was locked in the keystone of ecstasy" [1]

With its soaring lines, magnificent vaulting and vast quantities of fine carvings in the locally quarried golden limestone, Lincoln has long been regarded as the finest of our English Gothic cathedrals. John Ruskin wrote that it was "out and out, the most precious piece of architecture we possess", while Sacheverell Sitwell felt it worthy of the pharaohs. From the early fourteenth century until 1548 when the central spire of over 500ft had to be taken down, Lincoln Cathedral was the tallest building in the world, taller even than the Great Pyramid.

Watercolour painting of Lincoln Cathedral from the south west, by John Bangay, 1991
BY KIND PERMISSION OF THE ARTIST

It is not known exactly where the ancient Saxon cathedral of the See of Lindsey was situated and recent scholarship has discounted Stow Church, but after the Danish invasions, the See was moved to Dorchester.

William the Conqueror rewarded Remigius of Fecamp by making him the first Bishop of Lincoln, in 1072, having decided on the strategic importance of Lincoln. The See was transferred back from Dorchester, creating the largest diocese in England at that time.

Remigius's apsidal building with its huge three-arched West Front, suffered much structural damage, and between 1186 and 1200, Bishop Hugh of Avalon rebuilt it in the full Gothic style, with Master Geoffrey du Noyers and Master Richard as his architects. Superb vaults, (the one in the Choir with "syncopated" rib patterns which do not match from side to side), "optical illusion" wall arcades and much Purbeck marble shafting made for a very rich interior. The east end had radiating chapels, but these were pulled down in favour of a typically English square east end to house the great shrine of the canonised Hugh, whose cult was second only to that

[1] Reproduced by kind permission of Pollinger Limited and the Estate of Frida Lawrence-Ravagli.

of Thomas Becket. Master Simon of Thirsk, between 1256 and 1280, built this new "Angel Choir", which has been regarded as a high water mark of English Gothic architecture.

Lincoln's list of superlatives goes on. It has the largest West Front, with a unique Romanesque frieze of punishment and redemption, the largest Chapter House with a central column sending an explosion of ribs to the vault, and the tallest medieval central tower of any cathedral, rising to 271ft. Proving the immense distances covered by the Master Masons a column in the north east transept of massive, lobed, stone scrolls bursting between delicate shafts, is echoed by similar columns in the Norwegian cathedral of Trondheim.

Romantically inclined visitors are drawn to the tomb and story of Katherine Swynford, wife of John of Gaunt, or to the tomb of Queen Eleanor's heart. When she died in 1290, her heart and other viscera were left in Lincoln while her body travelled to London and its stopping places were marked by the famous Eleanor Crosses. Eleanor and her husband King Edward 1st had attended the consecration of St. Hugh's Angel Choir in 1280.

The Lincoln Imp, a horned, hairy demon above the northern column nearest to the East Window, became Lincolnshire's symbol and a local legend. But the most striking carvings of the interior are surely the angels in the spandrels of the Angel Choir with their musical instruments, or their biblical personages, or even holding the sun and moon.

John Harvey felt that Lincoln was the ideal place to see the aspirational quality of Gothic art, with every architectural element "beating against the sky". Echoing Ruskin and hosts of commentators ever since, Harvey concluded that Lincoln was a work of sublime imagination.

www.lincolncathedral.com

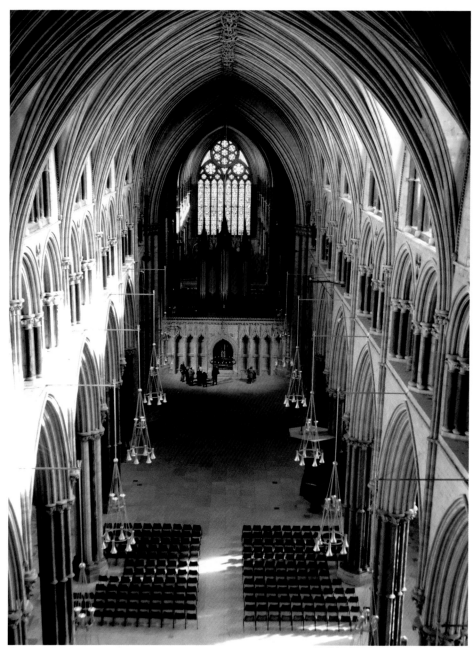

'Banks's View' of the interior of Lincoln looking east. Sir Joseph Banks, the great botanist, loved this view from the walkway high in the west end

FOTOLIA COPYRIGHT© MBFOLEY

LONDON ST. PAUL'S

S ir Christopher Wren's masterpiece of 1675-1710 had a great Gothic predecessor which perished in the Great Fire of London in 1666. Fortunately the Gothic cathedral was recorded in some detail by Wenceslaus Hollar (1607-77), the Scenographer Royal to King Charles II. His engravings were published by the antiquarian William Dugdale, in The History of St. Paul's Cathedral, 1658. As the part-Romanesque, part Early English cathedral was destroyed, Hollar watched it burn from his favourite vantage point, the tower of Southwark's St. Saviour's church, which was to become Southwark Cathedral.

Sadly the catalogue of losses at St. Paul's included a classical portico at the west end by Inigo Jones, of the 1630s, and other classical restoration work by him, on the exterior in particular. The portico was regarded as a masterpiece, and may have inspired Wren to build a larger, two-tiered version, for his complete rebuilding.

The See was established early in 604, with a Foundation of Secular Canons. Even before the Romans left, there had almost certainly been a church on Ludgate hill. St. Augustine installed Mellitus as Bishop of the East Saxons in a wooden cathedral in 604, but it burned down and almost a century later the first stone cathedral was built by St. Erkenwald but destroyed by the Vikings. It had contained

View into the Dome of St. Paul's Cathedral
COURTESY OF ST. PAUL'S CATHEDRAL

his shrine and was a place of pilgrimage. A new cathedral was destroyed by fire in 1087. The huge cathedral which replaced this was begun c.1090. The largest church in England, and largest north of the Alps, it was completed c.1350 and had a spire almost 500ft tall, taller than Salisbury's, but not as tall as Lincoln's.

The old Romanesque nave, twelve bays long and resembling Peterborough's, was rib vaulted in the early thirteenth century. It became famous as "St. Paul's walk" and was a mercantile space used for strolling and commerce.

New work on the choir began after 1251 and the old Norman work was remodelled with Purbeck marble giving a resemblance to contemporaneous work at Lincoln. The east end had a vast rose window 40ft across and unique in England. The Rood Screen at the Crossing was erected in the mid-fourteenth century and featured statues of eight English kings. It may have inspired the great screen at York, with its fifteen kings.

With its history of disastrous fires before the Great Fire, St. Paul's had acquired a classical external appearance thanks to Inigo Jones, long before the 34 year old Christopher Wren was entrusted with its rebuilding. Hollar's engravings are therefore of immense importance.

Wren's first design had no traditional nave, or aisles to the choir, but was dominated by a stupendous dome, very much as Michelangelo's design for St. Peter's in Rome had been. The Commissioners wanted traditional features of a Gothic cathedral, and Wren had to comply, but his dome still dominated, and was finished in 1710.

As a nephew of a bishop of Ely, Wren had been enthralled by Ely's Octagon and Lantern and wanted to repeat the effect in Baroque architectural language. The Baroque interior of St. Peter's is on a superhuman scale, whereas Wren's interior is altogether more beautiful and more dramatic as a poem of light and shade.

Outside and in, the genius of Grinling Gibbons can be seen in carvings of wood and stone, and his swags, ribbons and winged putti rejoice on the organ case. The great French ironworker Jean Tijou designed the glorious sanctuary gates. Wren intended more mosaics for his interior, but was again thwarted. Sir James Thornhill's Scenes from the Life of St. Paul, in the dome, are a reasonable compensation.

Although this is "the nation's church", with great monuments to the likes of the Duke of Wellington, one small item survived from the Gothic cathedral – the funeral effigy of its most famous Dean, the poet John Donne (1573-1631) who is seen in his winding sheet standing on an urn. Obsessed by death, he rehearsed this while being drawn by an artist. The sculptor of the effigy was Nicholas Stone.

In St. Paul's we have two great cathedrals in one, and Wenceslaus Hollar has ensured that we never forget the Gothic ancestor of Wren's masterpiece.

www.stpauls.co.uk

The Choir with the magnificent Baldacchino over the High Altar, consecrated in 1958
COURTESY OF ST. PAUL'S CATHEDRAL

NORWICH

Gothic cathedrals change their profiles dramatically as one walks around them and at Norwich, where the first view from the city centre is of a modest west front sinking away from the spectator, a walk to the south east unfolds a great cliff of a building soaring to an elegant spire atop the tallest Norman tower in England. The cathedral presides over a vast close from which traffic is banned, and tree-lined river walks arrive at Pull's Ferry and thence back to the cathedral again via peaceful rows of ancient houses.

Herbert de Losinga purchased the bishoprick from King William II "Rufus", and founded the cathedral in 1096 partly as an act of penance because his purchased status was then considered a grievous sin. The result, however, is a very beautiful building which stresses the gentle side of the Romanesque style.

The See had moved from Dunwich to Elmham and then to Thetford before coming to Norwich in 1094, and there was a community of sixty Benedictine monks. In 1119 Herbert de Losinga was buried in his cathedral, its magnificent nave and choir terminating in an ambulatory around the apse. This typically continental Romanesque apse was retained, and with the ancient bishop's throne behind the high altar, a sumptuous vault of 1472-99 by Robert Everard and glorious stained glass, it makes a very satisfying ensemble. An unusual reversal of zone sizes assists the effect – here, the triforium is taller than the arcades beneath, while the clerestory is almost double the height

Norwich Cathedral Spire and Labryinth from the Cloisters
COURTESY OF NORWICH CATHEDRAL

NORWICH *a personal pilgrimage*

of the triforium and was added by Robert Wodehirst, in the 1360s. The Presbytery and nave vaults, flying buttresses and spire are by Robert Everard, 1464-99. Second only to Salisbury, the spire is the third to be built on to the Norman tower.

Pevsner remarked that the interior is at its most powerful when one first sits down in the nave. He is right. Somehow, the Romanesque and Perpendicular styles speak the same language in a perfect marriage, and the entire church shimmers in a silver grey light. The beautiful roof bosses of Everard's Lierne vaults may be enjoyed by combining the use of binoculars and mirror tables.

There is a poignant reminder of 'Royal Norfolk' in the Cloisters. Among the niches there are figures of King George V and Queen Mary, and their son King George VI and his Queen, Elizabeth. In the wake of the recent success of the film 'The King's Speech', about George VI's battle with his speech impediment, these figures tell a double tale – all four loved Norfolk and Sandringham, and all suffered the effects of King Edward VIII's shortcomings and eventual Abdication in 1936.

The cloisters, which took more than a century to build, from 1297-1430, contain many outstanding bosses, amongst them the peculiar subject of King Nebuchadnezzar eating grass, and several green men, one quite clearly an entire face partly masked by gilded leaves and looking disturbingly alive. There is much fine Gothic tracery. Beyond the cloisters to the south is the dramatically glazed modern refectory from which fine views of the close and cathedral may be enjoyed.

Outside to the west, the ancient flint Erpingham and Ethelbert gates and the high wall mark the boundary between the Close and Tombland, a busy city area. Norwich Cathedral in its close is a place apart, and in a city bursting with fine historic churches it is by far the finest.

www.cathedral.org.uk

The ideal marriage of Romanesque and Perpendicular in the Nave of Norwich Cathedral
COURTESY OF NORWICH CATHEDRAL

OXFORD

We are on the old, local Oxford time as we enter Christ Church Cathedral, five minutes behind Greenwich Mean Time and a survival of pre-railway days, when local times all differed.

Oriented towards the sunrise on March 25th, Lady Day, in the early eighth century, the first building on this site had been a Saxon nunnery founded by St. Frideswide, according to legend a daughter of the King of Oxford.

She presided over twelve virgins of noble birth, having fended off the advances of King Algar of Leicester. She later cured him of blindness. She became Oxford's patron saint, and her shrine was placed in the Augustinian Priory which grew out of these early buildings.

The Priory of St. Frideswide was to continue until 1524 when Cardinal Wolsey successfully petitioned the Pope to dissolve it so that he could build a new college. As a result, three bays of the nave were demolished to make way for a large quadrangle, "Tom Quad".

Visitors to this somewhat truncated cathedral will not be dismayed, for they will

see a magnificent interior, culminating in a choir vault of such exotic splendour that many writers have regarded it as the finest of its type in England. This lierne vault has unusual lantern pendants, and Oxford's Divinity School has a similar vault designed by William Orchard, who died in 1504 and is buried in the cathedral. John Harvey gives the choir vault to him, with the dates 1478-1503.

The choir terminates visually in an Eastern chapel and wall designed by Sir George Gilbert Scott from 1869-76. His beautiful rose window, interlaced blind arcading and twin Romanesque windows below it are a triumph

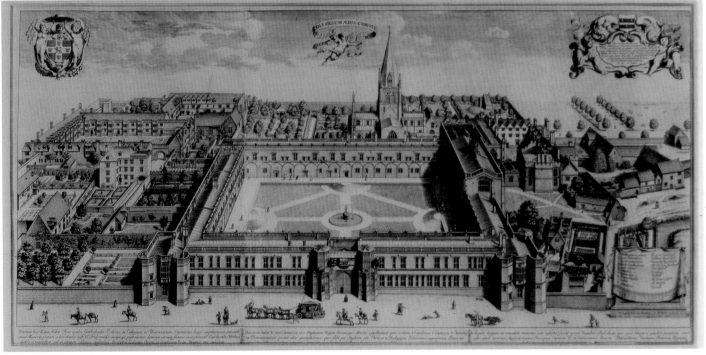

Old engraving of 'Tom Quad' with Christ Church Cathedral in the rear, by David Loggan, 1673
COURTESY OF CHRIST CHURCH CATHEDRAL, OXFORD

A 360° celebration of the interior of Oxford Cathedral
PHOTOGRAPH BY JASPER R. P. JOHNSON, 2011

of imaginative reconstruction, giving his idea of what this east end would originally have looked like. His restorations cost £24,000.

The main entrance to the cathedral is now via Tom Quad, where G.F. Bodley's Porch of 1872-3 cuts through the buildings in the quad to join the nave. The porch has never been liked, and has even been compared to a railway tunnel!

But a wonderful harmony exists between the surviving bays of the nave and the glorious choir, not least because the Norman columns continue throughout with Corinthian capitals and, unusually, a triforium arcade which is "dropped" below the arches of each bay, and held aloft by a lower arch, giving a feeling of greater height overall.

Several lovely windows of different dates and styles adorn the cathedral. The Chapel of St. Lucy has its "Becket window" of mid-fourteenth century glass telling the story of Thomas Becket, saved from destruction by the priests who removed the saint's face when

Henry VIII's commissioners were smashing such things on the King's orders. Great nineteenth century glass designers and makers are represented in windows by Edward Burne-Jones, William Morris, Clayton and Bell, and John Hardman, and there is some wonderful seventeenth century painted glass by the Flemish masters Abraham and Bernard van Linge, including Jonah seated with Gourds, beholding a vision of the city of Nineveh, in the north aisle.

The cathedral is also the college chapel of Christ Church. When Wolsey fell from favour, King Henry VIII refounded the new college in 1532, and created the diocese of Oxford ten years later, using as its centre the suppressed Oseney (or Osney) Abbey nearby. But the university and city grew in importance and in 1546 it was decided that the college chapel should become the cathedral of Christ the King, in a unique dual foundation. A further link with Wolsey can be seen in the superb Early English chapter house of 1225-50, for

below its east window is the foundation stone of Wolsey's intended grammar school at his birth place, Ipswich, which had been laid in 1528.

Other distinctive features include the much altered Latin Chapel of c.1350-55. Daily services were said here in Latin until 1648 and again after the restoration until 1861. Not to be missed is the wooden "watching loft", a perpendicular structure above a stone tomb and canopy, its exact use being the subject of debate. It is one of only two in existence, the other being in St. Alban's Cathedral. The early thirteenth century spire is one of the oldest in England, and rises to a 144ft.

Surprisingly, this is England's smallest medieval cathedral, but it proves conclusively that size isn't everything. The choir and east wall together constitute one of the most magnificent church interiors in England.

www.chch.ox.ac.uk/cathedral

OXFORD *a personal pilgrimage*

PETERBOROUGH

The shade of actor Donald Pleasance as the Rev. Septimus Harding will forever haunt the vast spaces of Peterborough Cathedral, which was chosen as the setting for the marvellous 1982 television adaptation of Anthony Trollope's first two Barchester novels. Built of strong Barnack limestone, Peterborough was begun in 1118, but two monasteries preceded it, the first destroyed by the Danes in 870, and the second built in 972 on the orders of King Edgar but destroyed by a fire in 1116 which burned for 9 days. The second monastery was one of Hereward the Wake's sanctuaries while he organised resistance to the Normans in the Fens.

Peterborough Cathedral, west front
COURTESY OF PETERBOROUGH CATHEDRAL

PETERBOROUGH *a personal pilgrimage*

DATE:

Approached from the south the cathedral has a powerful presence beyond the River Nene, but from the city it is lost behind modern developments so that the majesty of its West Front (1193-1230) comes as a surprise. Probably based on the three huge Romanesque openings in Lincoln's West Front, Peterborough's Gothic arches are unusual, for the central one is much narrower than the outer two. Obscuring the full effect of the central archway is a Perpendicular Galilee Porch of c.1375, an impertinent but pretty intruder which does not spoil the ensemble. Above all this, a riot of elaborate gables, pinnacles and spires prick and jab at the heavens. This West Front really is enjoying itself.

The Romanesque interior is more sobering. Considered second only to Durham, it has a similar building history, the choir and transepts coming first from 1118 when the place was founded by Abbot John of Sais, then the nave following on from 1155 to 1175. The west transept, a final widening of the nave leading to the West Front, was built between 1177 and 1193. Then in 1496 began the building, beyond the apsidal east end, of the Retro choir or Presbytery, thought to be by the great John Wastell (1485-1515) the architect of Kings' College Chapel, Cambridge. As with so many other English cathedrals, Peterborough thus opted for a square east end. The exotic splendours of the fan vaulting here provide a wonderful contrast with the severe Romanesque. The amazing painted roof of the nave and choir, beautifully restored, depicts a colourful array of early thirteenth century saints, kings, bishops and monsters of the medieval imagination,

Oliver Cromwell's soldiers destroyed the Chapter House, cloisters, stained glass and reredos, to say nothing of all the statues and the tomb of Catherine of Aragon, first wife of King Henry VIII, who died at Kimbolton in Huntingdonshire in 1536. Their divorce

The north aisle of Peterborough Cathedral –
Romanesque splendour
FOTOLIA COPYRIGHT©MBFOLEY

was the occasion of Henry's rift with Rome and when he dissolved the monasteries, Peterborough's Abbot John Chambers surrendered everything into the King's own hands and was immediately made the first Bishop.

Mary Queen of Scots was originally interred here after her execution at Fotheringhay Castle in 1587 but was reinterred in Westminster Abbey by her son King James I of England, in 1621.

Nurse Edith Cavell went to school in Peterborough and a memorial tablet from members of her old school celebrates this link with the woman who was shot for helping Belgian and French soldiers to escape from Belgium in the first World War.

There is one ancient carved stone of great importance, the Hedda Stone, once held to be a memorial to monks slaughtered by the Danes in 870 but now thought to be older. It is a priceless relic of Anglo-Saxon sculpture. The martyred King Oswald's arm was brought here into its own chapel but disappeared at the time of the Reformation.

Amongst modern contributions, the artist Alan Durst carved replacements for many statues on the West Front, and made the beautiful Annunciation for the chapel of the two saint daughters of King Penda of Mercia.

The year 2018 will see the cathedral's 900th anniversary and in the pipeline are a new Music School and Visitor Centre. With its outstanding features and historical associations, Peterborough Cathedral deserves many more visitors.

www.peterborough-cathedral.org.uk

RIPON

In Ripon Cathedral, we stand in the place where Christianity first came to northern England. Founded by St. Wilfrid and his monks in 675, the original building had a Saxon crypt, a part of which is all that now remains of the cathedral from which Wilfrid ruled the Diocese of the North, as Bishop of York. After the Danes had destroyed Wilfrid's cathedral, Benedictine monks rebuilt it, but this too was destroyed during William the Conqueror's "Harrying of the North" in 1069.

After St. Wilfrid's time, Ripon's status was as one of three Mother Churches of the great Archdiocese of York, with a college of secular canons.

From the third church, built by the first Norman Archbishop of York, Thomas of Bayeaux, monks set out to found nearby Fountains Abbey. Small traces of Thomas's building survive. The remaining history of Ripon Cathedral is complex.

Archbishop Roger, who supported King Henry II in his quarrels with Thomas Becket, built a fourth church, and the north transept, some of the north side of the choir, and the chapter house remain. There is a unique feature inside the chapter house. Two circular splayed windows throw light up into the roof.

Yet another rebuilding was undertaken by Archbishop Walter de Grey. The solid, four square West Front is his, and all the tall lancet windows once pointed towards two wooden spires on the squat towers. From 1288-97, the

The Central Tower of Ripon Cathedral from the south west, floodlit
COURTESY OF RIPON CATHEDRAL

east end of the choir was rebuilt, but the rest was not touched until 1482, after the central tower collapsed in 1450.

Ripon's unusual nave was the last part to be built. From c.1502, Christopher Scune, recorded as a Master Mason at Durham and the creator of Louth's famous Parish Church Spire, built for Ripon a nave of great dignity with enough interest in the arcade mouldings to make it beautiful. The wooden roof is suitably ribbed and pointed. Writers comment on a "might have been", had the elegant shafts

of the southern crossing pier been able to soar into a high Gothic arch, matched by a similar pier on the north side. It was not to be. We must imagine a triumphant pointed Crossing arch, which would have been a wonderful frame for the pointed arch and choir vaults beyond. It seems the money ran out. Scune's nave is plain compared with the many elaborate interiors of the same date, but it is reassuring, well proportioned and solid.

The sumptuous Choir is well hidden, really too well hidden, behind a York-style stone pulpitum with niched figures, and an organ case flanked by carved and pinnacled woodwork. We cannot yet see the great Geometrical East Window or Sir Ninian Comper's Reredos-Memorial to the men of Ripon who were killed in the First World War.

Entering the superb Perpendicular Choir, it is immediately obvious that it has one of the most lavish sets of stalls in England with wooden canopies rebuilt after 1660 when the spire fell from the central tower and wrought much damage internally. The misericords of c.1490 include Samson carrying off the Gates of Gaza, and four which feature a fox.

With Christopher Scune's great Crossing Arch incomplete, and evidence in every direction of the many rebuildings and of Sir George Gilbert Scott's restorations in the 1860s, Ripon is something of a "work in progress" – a concept which is valued today. John Harvey advised us to accept the patchwork nature of our cathedrals, and if you do this at Ripon you will find much to savour.

Ripon Minster became the Cathedral Church of St. Peter and St. Wilfrid in 1836.

www.riponcathedral.org.uk

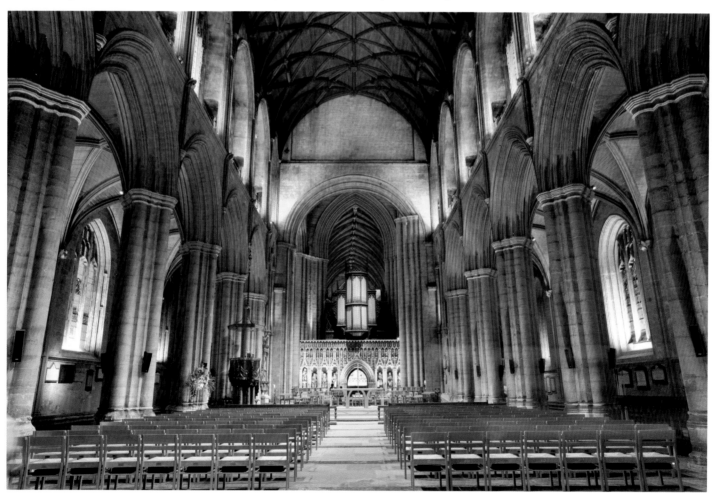

Christoper Scune's Nave in Ripon Cathedral
COURTESY OF RIPON CATHEDRAL

RIPON *a personal pilgrimage*

ROCHESTER

"Almost fallen to pieces with age" says an early chronicler of the first apsidal church built on the site, which lasted for at least 450 years. Today, Rochester Cathedral looks well cared for, and although it incorporates features of great age, they are also of great beauty and importance.

St. Augustine founded the See of Rochester in 604, only seven years after he founded the See of Canterbury, so Rochester Cathedral has the second longest history of any in England, and is the third church on the site with many additions and restorations. The Castle towers above the cathedral, overlooking the Medway and the west front. Both castle and cathedral were the work of Bishop Gundulph following the Norman Conquest, but today only the crypt survives. The apse of the first cathedral, meanwhile, is marked out in bronze in the nave. St. Paulinus and the first native-born English bishop, Ithamar, were buried in the first cathedral.

Two marvellous doorways will make any visit to Rochester Cathedral worthwhile. The West Door, a Norman portal of international importance, has an archway of five recessed orders and a tympanum carved in high relief

The Baptism Fresco by Sergei Fyodorov, 2003 in Rochester Cathedral
COPYRIGHT© DAVID ROBINSON

showing Christ in Majesty. The two column figures flanking the door are King Solomon and the Queen of Sheba. A characterful Romanesque frieze with statues of bishops flanks the portal. All of this animated stonework is of mid-twelfth century date.

Then there is the breathtaking doorway in the south east transept which once led into the narrow chapter house, now the library. Dating from the mid-fourteenth century, a lavishly crocketted ogee soars above a complex pointed arch, containing standing and seated figures and angels sheltered beneath miniature canopies and all set against a richly pinnacled and crocketted backcloth of patterned stonework. It is a virtuoso display, which cannot be missed.

Otherwise, wall paintings on the choir walls are the beguiling features of an interior which rather lacks architectural excitement – although the gradual ascent to the High Altar does have a drama of its own. There are heraldic panels with gold lions and fleur de lys, a big Wheel of Fortune, with strenuous figures turning it, and you can almost hear it grinding. These were painted to commemorate King Edward III's victories over the French.

The Romanesque nave is light and satisfying in itself, with ornament on each arch to save it from plainness. The nave joins the crossing rather clumsily, with a huge arch which seems too wide for its somewhat depressed height.

In the north nave transept, continuing the tradition of wall paintings in true fresco technique into wet plaster, the Russian artist Sergei Fyodorov completed in 2003 a fresco on the theme baptism, to commemorate the Millennium. This is thought to be the first instance of fresco painting in an English church for five hundred years, and the artist attracted crowds while working, and spent many weeks in search of ideal plaster and pigment mixtures. At the other end of the timescale, there is in the crypt a graffito of the twelfth century, showing a saint gently protecting two people.

Charles Dickens, the great Victorian novelist who lived nearby, is commemorated with a memorial tablet.

The cathedral was restored by Sir George Gilbert Scott from 1871 and by John Loughborough Pearson from 1892, but otherwise we are swept far away to the world of the great French Romanesque cathedrals and their mighty portals, as we savour a West Front of international stature.

www.rochestercathedral.org

Rochester Cathedral Library door (formerly to the Chapter House)

ST. ALBANS

All distant views of St. Albans are impressive. The cathedral looks enormous, and is exceeded in length only by Winchester while its central tower seems a lot taller than its 144ft. It had been the first monastery in England, uniquely built from Roman bricks from the city of Verulamium.

In 209, a Briton living in Verulamium gave sanctuary to a Christian priest on the run from persecution. This brave gesture, followed by the conversion and baptism of the Briton, whose name was Alban, resulted in his death by beheading, for he had swapped clothing with the priest when the Roman soldiers came, and in front of the magistrates, he proclaimed his belief in the living God.

Alban became England's native Christian martyr, and a small church appeared on the site of his martyrdom five hundred years before an abbey was founded, probably by Offa, King of Mercia. It was enormous but there are no traces of it today. The present cathedral is mainly Norman, by the first Norman abbot, Paul of Caen, from 1077 to 1115.

In the thirteenth century the Benedictine abbey had become wealthy so stone was brought in for massive extensions east and west, and a new west front was started, with flanking towers, but these were never built.

The West Front through which we enter today was the gift of the wealthy First Baron Grimthorpe who from 1877 paid for much needed improvements to what had become a Parish Church (surely the biggest in England) in the wake of the 1539 Dissolution and

St. Alban's Cathedral central tower from the south

destruction of all the abbey buildings. 1877 saw the formation of the new diocese of Hertfordshire and Bedfordshire, and St. Albans was the natural choice for cathedral. Baron Grimthorpe seems to have wanted a rival to York's Five Sisters window because he had five immense lancets introduced into the south transept.

John Betjeman urged us to experience the "overwhelming massiveness desired by the conquering Normans" by standing in the nave. Here, as he said, the arches seem cut into the thick walls as into solid rock. The medieval murals on the piers were originally related to a series of side altars and took fifty years to restore. On the west side of the piers they show the crucifixion above and the Blessed Virgin Mary below, while on the south are saints including St. Christopher, St. Thomas Becket, and St. Edward the Confessor. St. Thomas's face has, as usual, been obliterated by Henry VIII's Commissioners.

The thirteenth century timber vault over the Choir (1420-40) has painted patterns executed during the Abbacy of John of Wheathampstead. Thus we see the eagle and the lamb of St. John the Evangelist, and St. John the Baptist, in foliated roundels.

In the Sanctuary, the beautifully carved Shrine of St. Alban shows his martyrdom, while a carved wooden watching chamber looks upon it. Oxford Cathedral has the only other watching chamber of this type. No one can miss the huge stone rood screen, a breathtakingly detailed Perpendicular masterpiece with elaborate canopies and Christ Crucified at the centre. This late fourteenth century screen has carved figures of the 1890s, funded by Lord Aldenham. The fine Reredos backing the High Altar is the work of Sir Alfred Gilbert.

In 1539 the Chapter House was demolished, but in 1982 the Queen opened a new one of brick chosen to blend with the abbey, by William Whitfield. The extensive Green to the south is very pleasant and affords dramatic views, but it was once the first monastery in England, with buildings around four quadrangles.

www.stalbanscathedral.org

The Choir of St. Alban's Cathedral looking to the High Altar
COPYRIGHT© ST. ALBAN'S CATHEDRAL

ST. ALBANS *a personal pilgrimage*

SALISBURY

Salisbury Cathedral will forever be associated with the paintings of John Constable RA (1776-1837) who made it famous as a symbol of hope surviving the most violent of storms. It was built in a single campaign from 1220 to 1258 when it was consecrated. Then came the completion of the West Front, the cloisters, the Chapter House and the great Spire, the finest and highest in England at 404ft. All was complete by 1310.

Salisbury's remarkably untroubled building history came about because Bishop Richard Poore's new cathedral did not need to conform to the site or ruins of previous ones. They had been built at Old Sarum nearby, the huge Iron Age hill fort which became a Roman garrison and a major Saxon fortress. The Conqueror built a castle there, and the cathedral of the new Diocese of Sarum (made from the Diocese of Sherborne and Ramsbury) was also begun and enlarged by the powerful Bishop Roger between 1102 and 1139. But Old Sarum went into decline very gradually and returned to grass, and that is why Bishop Poore petitioned the Pope for the building we see today.

The interior of this perfectly proportioned building is a classic case of Early English architecture on a diet, for the columns and shafts seem so slim, perhaps because of the amount of daylight flooding in. This interior allows us to perform a creative act of the imagination, aided by the words of George Gilbert Scott, who while restoring the place

Salisbury Cathedral from the south west
COPYRIGHT© ASH MILLS

with his father, Sir Gilbert Scott, found a lot of colour beneath all the white wash.

"The intention (was) to have…richly coloured wall spaces, the walls painted red, relieved by bold scroll work in black, and the mouldings were decorated upon the same system".

The glass originally included much grisaille or silver grey so the entire colour-light scheme would have been harmonised.

During the Reformation, Salisbury's stained glass was destroyed, but the want of colour is being supplied, and in 1980 a rich example, designed by Gabriel Loire in his workshops

near Chartres, was dedicated in the Trinity Chapel. It is the "Prisoners of Conscience" window and it features anxious, watchful faces peering from that same colour combination which we see in the finest early medieval glass – deep blues, reds, turquoise, green and gold, harmonised by a little white.

Fortunately too, we can see today the red-black mouldings of the vault ribs and some painted medallions on the vault of the Choir Transept, and here also are strainer arches similar to the scissor arches at Wells but minus the central "portholes". These arches were deemed necessary to arrest the collapse of the spire and tower.

The architects or Master Masons at Salisbury deserve a roll-call. Elias of Dereham and Nicholas of Ely built the Lady Chapel, Choir, Great Transept and Nave, then Richard Mason built the West Front, Cloisters and Chapter House. Richard Farleigh built the tower and spire from 1334-1380.

Salisbury Cathedral has one of the loveliest and most sweeping of all English Closes, with lawns, tall trees and houses of high quality such as the early eighteenth century Mompesson House. The cathedral can satisfyingly be taken in at a single glance. The noble two-tiered tower, turrets and banded spire, the elegant elongated flying buttresses, and the festive west front all climb to the sky in sublime unity. There is one more bonus, for anyone wishing to know exactly what the detached bell tower looked like before its destruction by Wyatt, in 1798, could refer to the lovely plate by Hollar in Dugdale's Monasticon volume three of 1673. There it stood on the north side of the close, with a little spire of its own, like a three-tiered wedding cake.

www.salisburycathedral.org.uk

Interior of Salisbury Cathedral from the west
PHOTO ASH MILLS

SOUTHWARK

The oldest Gothic church in London, Southwark Cathedral now has a superb range of new facilities in its Millennium Buildings opened in April 2001 by the great Nelson Mandela. Before the Reformation the site had been an Augustinian priory whose canons built a hospital at the gates and named it after St. Thomas of Canterbury. He stayed at the priory on his return from exile before proceeding to Canterbury. At that time, Southwark was in the Diocese of Winchester. Long before, in 606, a legend told of one Mary, daughter of a ferryman, who founded a religious house here. Then in 1086 the Domesday Book recorded a monastery and a college of priests.

In the Elizabethan period, the Priory of St. Mary Overie (Anglo-Saxon Ofer or "by the bankside") as it had been called before the Reformation, became the parish church of St. Saviour's, for the whole of theatrical Bankside, with its many actors' names appearing in the parish registers. Shakespeare is commemorated, and a window depicts characters from his plays. His brother Edmond's funeral took place here in 1607. The actor Edward Alleyne is commemorated, and dramatists John Fletcher and Philip Massenger are buried here along with Philip Henslowe, owner of the Rose Theatre. Today, the reconstructed Globe Theatre stands near, brain child of America's Sam Wanamaker, who sadly died before it opened to the public.

Architecturally, Southwark is a gem. The lower stage of the famous chequered and white, pinnacled tower was designed by Henry Yevele in c.1385. Hailed by Alec Clifton Taylor as "purest Early English", the five-bay choir has a noble clerestory of triple openings to each bay while the light, delicate retrochoir is even earlier, c.1208. Both are by Richard Mason. This eastern arm of the cathedral is perfectly complemented by a very atmospheric nave which seems original but was in fact the work of Sir Arthur Blomfield between 1889 and 1897, after the original nave had been demolished. With London's population expanding, Southwark was ideally sited to become the cathedral of the new Diocese of Southwark, in 1905.

It seems that the word, written, spoken or acted, has been central to the purpose of this cathedral. The links with many actors, the fact that Bishop Lancelot Andrewes was one of the translators of the King James Bible, and the grave of the medieval poet and friend of Chaucer, John Gower, all prove the point, as

The Millennium Buildings & Courtyard, Southwark Cathedral
REPRODUCED WITH THE KIND PERMISSION OF THE DEAN & CHAPTER OF SOUTHWARK

The Choir and Nave of Southwark Cathedral
REPRODUCED WITH THE KIND PERMISSION OF THE DEAN & CHAPTER OF SOUTHWARK

indeed does the use of this cathedral by the Queen for a recent Christmas broadcast which was the first to be recorded away from the Royal Palaces.

Words are tools of learning, and here in 1607, John Harvard was baptised. Arriving in Massachusetts in 1637, he died of consumption but left his library and half his fortune for the new Harvard College. In the twentieth century, Harvard graduate Oscar Hammerstein II became a great admirer of English Choral music and gave the cathedral choir an endowment allowing two boys to be taken on as Hammerstein Chanters. A Harvard Chapel commemorates John Harvard and was furnished by Sir Ninian Comper, who did a lot of work for the cathedral including the East Window, in the 1930s.

The atmosphere of cloisters, such a boon in the ceaseless commercial roar of the cathedral's surroundings, is brilliantly conveyed in the new Millennium Buildings, which comprise conference rooms, a shop and a refectory in well-lit and buttressed elevations bordering a courtyard complete with shrubs and trees – an oasis in a very welcoming place.

cathedral.southwark.anglican.org

SOUTHWARK *a personal pilgrimage*

SOUTHWELL

There is a gentleness in the name Southwell which is echoed in the architecture of its beloved Minster. Built of creamy Mansfield Stone, its Romanesque nave is friendly rather than forbidding, while its famous Chapter House is only half the size of most. Yet there are unexpected superlatives in Southwell which will enchant those who long to be taken back in time.

The Parish Church of St. Mary the Virgin became a cathedral in 1884 when a new diocese was made for parts of Derbyshire and Nottinghamshire. An early nineteenth century restoration by local architect Richard Ingeleman brought new assembly rooms, a residence for the Chapter, and a grammar school. Then in the 1880s Ewan Christian (1814-95) who had transformed Carlisle Cathedral, rebuilt the two pyramidal steeples on the west towers. These are a striking surprise, and are not English in feeling, but rather of the continental Romanesque as though we could be in Tournai, Conques or Cluny.

The nave is atmospheric, almost breathing the air of the twelfth century. Stocky columns and round arches support a clearly defined second tier of more elaborate squat columns and arches, topped in turn by an equally clearly defined row of clerestory openings, which on the outside form an unusual row of round windows. The overall effect is of two Roman aqueducts (truly Romanesque!) and at the crossing, huge round arches frame the view into the choir past the organ case on the stone

J. M. W. Turner's wash study of Southwell from the north-west, 1794
BY KIND PERMISSION OF THE DEAN AND CHAPTER OF SOUTHWELL MINSTER

pulpitum screen. Together, the western towers, nave and transepts offer a pure experience of basic Romanesque architecture.

The "Leaves of Southwell" are the world famous carvings of naturalistic leaves and flowers which are found inside the Chapter House and its passageway. Here is the English countryside in stone, carved around the beginning of the fourteenth century. Pevsner, following Professor Seward, lists a dizzying array, dominated by maple leaves, and followed by oak, hawthorn, ranunculus, potentilla, vine, ivy, hops, rose, briony, mulberry, hemp nettle, and (possibly) fig, geranium, wormwood, bitter

sweet, cherry and blackthorn. Try to find the dragons playing in foliage in the passageway, and a hare with hounds inside the Chapter House. Many of these carvings seem blown by a breeze, and all illustrate the words of Vincent of Beauvais:

"I am moved with spiritual sweetness towards the creator and ruler of this world when I behold the magnitude and beauty and permanence of his creation."

John Betjeman rightly remarked that in Southwell, a perfect balance is achieved between the discipline of Early English architecture and the new freedom of naturalistic ornament.

Southwell's ancient treasures include tessellated paving and an eleventh century Tympanum or carved doorway lintel, showing St. Michael and a dragon and David rescuing a lamb from a lion. These are thought to be from the first church on the site built in 956. There is also the Shrine of St. Eadburgh, a Royal lady whose piety was legendary in the history of the Saxon church.

Not to be missed, either, are the superb misericord carvings in the choir, which is entered through the glorious triple arched pulpitum screen, a masterpiece of the Decorated style.

On leaving, surely no visitor could fail to notice the majestic West Window, an enormous seven light Perpendicular structure of c.1450 now filled with glass designed by Patrick Reyntiens and made by Keith Barley in 1996. Here is the Heavenly Host of Angels, truly angels of light, with seven of them holding the Acts of Creation. It is Southwell's final, thrilling flourish.

www.southwellminster.org

The Romanesque Nave of Southwell looking east
BY KIND PERMISSION OF THE DEAN AND CHAPTER OF SOUTHWELL MINSTER

WELLS

The tranquillity of ancient England untroubled by the roar of traffic, can be savoured at Wells more readily than anywhere else. And in the mirror waters of the moat around the Bishop's Palace, this "Queen of Cathedrals" can be seen in a perfect reflection. The arresting West Front faces the visitor down a huge lawn. It achieves that ideal English balance between soaring vertical buttresses and horizontal zones of sculpture, originally over three hundred statues and reliefs of which around half remain, to represent the Fall and Redemption of Man, from the creation to the Enthronement of Christ. A few are newer replacements, but the deterioration in the originals was beyond repair. Thomas Norreys (1229-49) was the Master Mason, with William Wynford (1360-1403) credited with the perpendicular tower stages.

The Central Tower of 1315-22 perhaps by Thomas Witney (1316-42) is a Perpendicular masterpiece and as soon as it was completed, it began to slip. Master Mason William Joy (1329-46) may have been the genius who decided to build three huge pointed arches across the crossing piers to the nave and transepts, topped by three inverted identical arches and with portholes in the side spaces. The effect is that of three pairs of stone scissors,

Wells Cathedral from the west front
COURTESY OF WELLS CATHEDRAL

the thrust of the tower being in the event, transferred around these bracing shapes, and finally brought to the earth. Betjeman felt that these unique strainer arches held "the most thrilling fluency of Gothic space, pulling all parts of the church visually together".

The first See of Wells created in 909, grew out of an early eighth century church traditionally founded by St. Aldhelm, Bishop of Sherbourne. Bishop Robert of Lewes (1136-66) built the first Norman cathedral of which supposedly only the font remains. Bishop Robert obtained the reinstatement of Wells in the designation of the See after his predecessor John de Villula had taken it exclusively for Bath (see entry on Bath Abbey). Bishop Reginald de Bohun began building the present cathedral around 1175 and it became the first entirely Gothic cathedral, without any of the usual Romanesque survivals.

Looking like an advancing sea of golden stone as it joins into one from two tributaries, the staircase leading to the beautiful octagonal Chapter House and the Vicar's Hall must have been photographed countless times, but never more poetically than by Frederick Evans (1853-1943) who toured English cathedrals to record the life and drama of their stonework. Like Lincoln's enormous chapter house the one at Wells has a central column and was built c.1293-1310.

Wells and Salisbury have the two earliest surviving fourteenth century clocks in the country, and on the quarter hour the figure of Jack Blandiver kicks the quarters with his heels followed by knights on horseback, one being thrown from his horse at each turn. While it is lovely to connect with medieval times by experiencing such unusual performances, we can also appreciate how finely carved the West Front must have been by visiting the capitals of the south transept, which show a kaleidoscope of medieval behaviour. Similar scenes occur in the famous Luttrell Psalter, and at Wells too, these capitals portray the catching of a thief in an orchard, and people suffering various afflictions.

There is one more feature at Wells which connects us with the medieval glaziers, carpenters and masons. The making of plans and templates went on in a "trasour" or tracing house, and the one at Wells is in the chamber over the North Porch. Its plaster floor is covered with incised lines drawn by the craftsmen. York also has a tracing house.

Whether stone has been lovingly carved into human, plant or animal forms, or made into a miracle of precision engineering like the scissor arches, Wells offers the entire spectrum on a human scale, which has made it a greatly loved, and fiercely championed cathedral.

www.wellscathedral.org.uk

Wells Cathedral Scissor Arches
COURTESY OF WELLS CATHEDRAL

Wells Cathedral Chapter House steps
COURTESY OF WELLS CATHEDRAL

WESTMINSTER ABBEY

King Henry III reigned from 1216-72, and he was the greatest royal champion of the Gothic style and a great builder of churches. Westminster Abbey was his finest achievement, for he rebuilt it in order to give his favourite saint, Edward the Confessor, a magnificent shrine.

Work began in 1245 under his Mason Henry of Reyns. John of Gloucester took over in 1253-4 and may have introduced the ridge rib, that most English of Gothic features and unusual in such a tall French-Gothic building. Behing the High Altar, Edward the Confessor's remains were sumptuously interred. Beyond was a French "chevet" of radiating chapels, bar tracery deriving for Rheims and a polygonal apse.

The Benedictine abbey, founded by Edward the Confessor in 1065, must have been very different. William the Conqueror was crowned there on Christmas Day 1066 and ever since, Westminster Abbey has been the Coronation Church. Only two monarchs were never actually crowned, Edward V and Edward VIII. Many monarchs are buried here, up to King George II who died in 1760. King Henry V and Queen Elizabeth I have especially fascinating tombs.

King Henry VII, anxious to emphasise his Lancastrian heritage, decided to create a worthy resting place at the abbey for his favourite martyr, King Henry VI, who had predicted the Tudor King's future. Thus, the Lady Chapel was pulled down to provide for an

Westminster Abbey – French Gothic magnificence on the North Transept
FOTOLIA COPYRIGHT© STEPHEN FINN

impressive new chapel for the shrine of Henry VI, whose remains were at Windsor.

A furious row broke out about the custody of the relics, and the coffin remained, in the end, at Windsor, leaving Henry VII with a stunning chapel which was so entirely his, that he left orders in his will for someone to create a tomb for himself, his wife and his mother.

From Sir Reginald Bray's plans, Robert Vertue completed the chapel from c.1503-19 with a magnificent pendant fan vault and elaborate flying buttresses outside. The Florentine sculptor Pietro Torrigiano executed the monument, with the bronze recumbent effigies of the King and Queen, Elizabeth.

Westminster Abbey became a cathedral in 1540 by Royal Decree of King Henry VIII, but this status lasted only a decade. Gradually the abbey became the repository of tombs and monuments to many great English men and women. Sir Isaac Newton, Geoffrey Chaucer and Ben Jonson are here, and "Poets' Corner" has become famous. In "Innocents' Corner", lie the remains of the two little princes murdered in the Tower and the daughters of King James I, one only 3 days old. A famous prize fighter called Broughton is buried in the west walk of the cloisters. He posed for the figure of Hercules on Sir Peter Warren's monument in the north transept.

Although tombs and often outrageous marble monuments are everywhere, somehow the majestic Gothic linearity of Henry III's great interior wins the day, with its Purbeck marble columns and soaring vault. Even Sir Christopher Wren's famous western towers, begun in 1722, pale into insignificance when we stand by the Tomb of the Unknown Warrior, and gaze at the highest vault in England which has sheltered so many glittering events in our history.

www.westminster-abbey.org

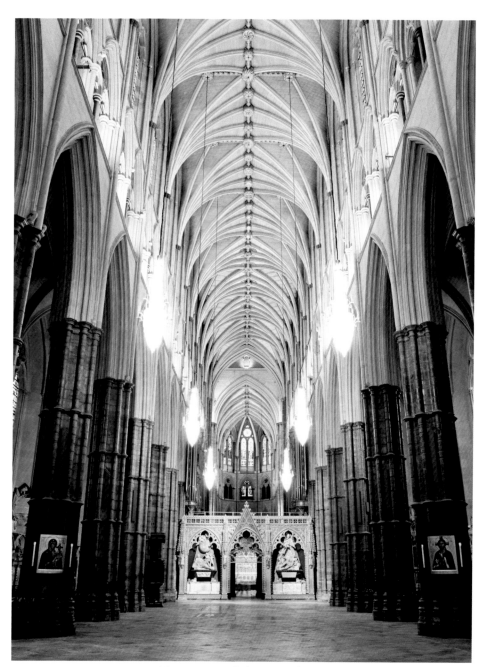

Westminster Nave looking east and vault

WINCHESTER

Resting on the stone screens of the Presbytery of Winchester Cathedral, are the mortuary chests of the Danish King Canute, his Queen Emma, and many Saxon kings and bishops. William the Conqueror's second and third sons, Richard de Bernay and King William "Rufus", who both met their end while hunting in the New Forest, are also interred in this vast cathedral, which is the longest Gothic church in Europe, at 554ft.

Winchester was the old Saxon capital of England and in Norman times remained one of the two largest principal cities, with a very rich diocese extending from the south bank of the Thames to the south coast. Even the church which preceded the present one was probably the largest Romanesque church in Europe, and the Norman masonry remains in the north and south transepts.

Approached from the city across a green, the exterior is unremarkable, save for the elegant West Front of c.1360, but inside, we see perhaps the stateliest of interiors, with a glorious eleven-bay nave and a choir beneath the central tower. The vaults are richly sculpted and vigorous lierne ribs house an explosion of bosses which seem like hundreds of flower heads. William Wynford (fl.1360-1403) was chiefly responsible for this Perpendicular masterpiece, built for Bishop William of Wykeham (1367-1404).

The first church on the site was built in 648 by King Cenwalh, but even earlier in 635, King Kynegils of Wessex was baptised here in

Winchester Cathedral from the west, in the snow
PHOTO BY JOE LOW, REPRODUCED BY KIND PERMISSION OF THE CHAPTER OF WINCHESTER

his capital city. The See was removed from Dorchester to Winchester c.679. There are no remains of this first cathedral of Wessex, nor of the second, but here we come to Winchester's two watery connections, for the second cathedral housed the remains of Bishop Swithun, who in his humility refused to be buried inside his church, but was taken inside after his death. When his grave was opened to allow this on July 15th 971, rain fell – for forty days. The Chronicles tell us that it was the Heavens weeping for Swithun, and that is the origin of the famous piece of weather lore.

The second watery connection involved William Walker, the hero-diver, who from 1906 to 1912 worked in 14ft of water, mainly beneath the foundations of the retrochoir, as he replaced a peat bed with almost 115,000 concrete blocks and 25,800 bags of concrete. The cathedral has a bronze statue of him, for he saved the building from collapse.

The cathedral we see today was begun by Bishop Walkelin, a Norman who succeeded the Anglo-Saxon Stigand in 1070. It began with a crypt and transepts, and it was felt that a grander shrine was needed for the remains of St. Swithun. In 1107 the great tower collapsed, and the transepts had to be rebuilt.

It is understandable that William of Wykeham (1367-1404), Winchester's greatest

The Crypt of Winchester Cathedral,
with a bronze figure by Antony Gormley,
called 'Found II'

PHOTO BY JOE LOW,
REPRODUCED BY KIND PERMISSION OF THE CHAPTER OF WINCHESTER

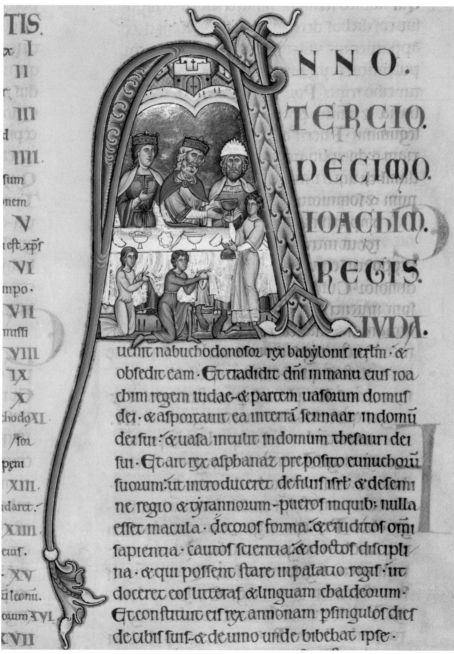

A page from the illuminated Winchester Bible

PHOTO BY JOE LOW, REPRODUCED BY KIND PERMISSION OF THE CHAPTER OF WINCHESTER

and most powerful bishop, would wish to rebuild his cathedral in the latest and most English of the Gothic styles, the Perpendicular. While he is buried in splendour in the nave, the equally splendid tomb of Cardinal Beaufort, four times Chancellor of England, stands in the retrochoir, and in 1923 after the canonisation of Joan of Arc, a statue of her was put opposite, making the point that Beaufort had been instrumental in condemning her to death.

No literary pilgrim would want to miss the tombs of the great Jane Austen in the north aisle, or of Izaak Walton, author of "The Compleat Angler". Austen's black grave slab is beautifully worded.

Finally in this brief appreciation, Winchester's famous twelfth century illuminated Bible must be mentioned. Christopher de Hamel has declared it to be the greatest work of art produced in England. Now in four volumes, its stunning illuminations were thought to have been executed by six artists, and the phenomenal cost was probably borne by Henry of Blois, brother of King Stephen and a bishop of Winchester.

winchester-cathedral.org.uk

WORCESTER

A window in the north wall of Worcester Cathedral illustrates "The Dream of Gerontius" and commemorates its composer Sir Edward Elgar (1857-1934) who was born at Broadheath nearby. Worcester was his favourite cathedral and its vast Early English spaces provide a superb acoustic. The cathedral has since echoed to many of his works.

Built of dark red sandstone, Worcester is one of the most splendid examples of the Early English style which began to stress the linear and the rhythmical in Gothic architecture.

The diocese was created in 680 when the first cathedral had been consecrated. In 961 Bishop Dunston, who became Archbishop of Canterbury, inaugurated with the help of his successor, Oswald, a Benedictine monastery which was also on the site of the present building. Oswald's piety led to his canonisation and although his cathedral now leaves no trace, many pilgrims visited his shrine. In 1062 Bishop Wulstan began a long reign and of his cathedral, only the huge Norman crypt remains. It is one of the finest crypts in existence and has an ambulatory around its east end so that pilgrims to the shrine of St. Oswald could move around more easily. Wulstan was made a saint in 1203. Above ground, the cathedral we see today was built between c.1224 and 1395.

The cathedral's sandstone had decayed so badly by the mid-nineteenth century that an almost total resurfacing was necessary, and from 1857-1874, the nave, floor, west door, pulpit, choir screen, Bishop's throne and reredos were all heavily restored or newly installed, under the leadership of A.E. Perkins and then Sir George Gilbert Scott. All this work was so beautifully done that while the exterior seems rather harsh, the interior celebrates its architecture enhanced by Victorian roof paintings in the choir and a reredos behind the High Altar, which deserves an accolade.

Standing before the High Altar in Worcester must be a high point for any lover of the Victorian Gothic, for the great reredos with Christ the King and the Four Evangelists was designed by Sir George Gilbert Scott in 1871. Together with the elaborate screen and soaring shafts of the great east window beyond, Scott's majestic figures take command and preside over one of the most lavish Gothic spectacles in any English cathedral.

Whether King John, whose tomb stands before all this, was worthy of it, is a matter of debate. He was, admittedly, once flanked by the shrines of St. Oswald and St. Wulfram, and he did choose to be buried here, in 1216. His recumbent effigy is the earliest of the Royal effigies in England. In an attempt to lend him

Worcester Cathedral from the bridge on the River Severn with 2 narrowboats
REPRODUCED WITH THE KIND PERMISSION OF THE DEAN & CHAPTER OF WORCESTER CATHEDRAL

a little more holiness perhaps, two Bishops approach his back and shake their censers.

Among the most beautiful chantry chapels in England is that of Prince Arthur, the elder brother of King Henry VIII, who at only 15 was married to Catherine of Aragon, and went to live in Ludlow Castle where he sadly died within three months. Two years later, Catherine famously married Henry VIII. In Arthur's Chapel can be found carvings of the Portcullis of the House of Lancaster, the Tudor Rose, and the Falcon and Fetterlock of the House of York. The writhing lierne vaulting has pendants and feels almost prickly with energy.

The ashes of Stanley Baldwin, Prime Minister at the time of the Abdication of King Edward VIII are interred in the cathedral.

Of the Master Masons who gave us Worcester Cathedral, Alexander Mason, William of Shockerwick and John Clyve must be singled out. Clyve (fl.1362-92) did much of the interior, the chapter house and the cloisters, and also perhaps the superb tower which is beautifully proportioned and makes a tremendous impression from a distance beyond the River Severn. These men have given us a very atmospheric building, which seems to culminate in Scott's reredos. He was paid ten guineas for it, but he has given us a celestial vision beyond price.

www.worcestercathedral.co.uk

The interior of Worcester Cathedral, looking east

REPRODUCED WITH THE KIND PERMISSION OF THE DEAN & CHAPTER OF WORCESTER CATHEDRAL

YORK

Beckoning at the far end of that famous ancient street, The Shambles, York Minster is the inevitable climax of a city which, with all its historic attractions, seems entirely given over to tourism.

The scale and magnificence of the Minster and its famous "Five Sisters" window have invited palatial superlatives, and the late Victorian social reformer Edward Carpenter even referred to "the great, grey Alps" of columns in the nave in his poem "York Minster". The East Window, its glass approaching the quality of glass in Chartres Cathedral, is reinforced by a carved stone grid in front and is the largest expanse of medieval painted glass anywhere, by Hugh Hedon, 1400-5.

The See of York was established in 627 with a foundation of secular canons. Edwin of Northumbria was baptised by Paulinus in York in that year, and Pope Gregory decreed that York should be the missionary church for the North of England, dedicated to St. Peter. With Canterbury's See established in 597, also with an archbishop, the primacy of both Sees was fought over in a very unseemly manner for many centuries, until Pope Innocent VI, in the fourteenth century, decreed that the Archbishop of York should be "Primate of England", while the Archbishop of Canterbury should be "Primate of ALL England".

The present cathedral, founded by Archbishop Walter de Grey (1216-55) was built gradually as an older one was demolished. Thomas, Bishop of Bayeaux, had been appointed by the Conqueror as his first Norman archbishop, and he drew up a set of rules for the government of all non-monastic

York Minster
REPRODUCED WITH THE KIND PERMISSION OF THE DEAN AND CHAPTER OF YORK MINSTER

cathedrals, which formed the basis of the running of those cathedrals founded by secular canons. Nothing survives above ground of Thomas's cathedral, yet even in 1328, his choir still existed, and hosted the wedding of King Edward III to Philippa of Hainault. Between 1407-23 William Colchester built the central tower and William Hyndeley made the vault beneath it, c.1470, which is greatly admired today.

The Crypt of c.1154-81 is wonderful to see because it contains the foundations of Thomas of Bayeaux's cathedral and some superb incised Romanesque columns in the style of Durham.

Massive steel and concrete foundations ensure the stability of the central tower and were introduced by Bernard Fielden in 1967.

York may not have the symphonic richness of stonework or vaulting enjoyed by Exeter or Lincoln, but its elaborate stone screen by William Hyndeley (1475-1500) is unforgettable, displaying the fifteen English kings from William I to Henry VI. Their statues occupy seven niches to the north, and eight to the south of the entrance to the choir. This hardly noticeable imbalance is so typical of English Gothic and in so many of our cathedrals, the north side hardly ever matches the south side.

Large cathedral windows almost always have names, and York has its famous "Five Sisters" and the "Heart of Yorkshire". Each lancet of the Five Sisters is 50ft tall by 5ft wide, and each has gently toned grey-green floral patterning with red and blue highlights. The West Window has at its core a beautiful heart shaped tracery, hence the "Heart of Yorkshire".

Unusually, the nave still has all of its original glass. Begun in c.1290, the spacious nave spans 58ft, thought too dangerous to vault in stone, so a wooden roof was built and from this a wooden vault was suspended, and rendered in plaster. The height to the apex is 102ft, very tall for an English cathedral. The fine Early English Chapter House (1286-96) has no need of a central column because it, too, has a wooden vault.

John Betjeman rightly felt that the passageway from the north transept into the Chapter House was the most beautiful walk through stained glass in England, but the most dramatic spatial experience at York must be the Crossing and Undertower which works as a breathtaking space forcing the eye forever upward, to move from the gorgeous undertower vaulting to the completely restored roof of the south transept which was destroyed by fire on July 9, 1984.

Cathedral fires are by no means exclusive to the medieval period!

www.yorkminster.org

The Great Transept of York Minster, illuminated from the south
REPRODUCED WITH THE KIND PERMISSION OF THE DEAN AND CHAPTER OF YORK MINSTER

The Nave of York Minster looking west to 'the heart of Yorkshire' window
REPRODUCED WITH THE KIND PERMISSION OF THE DEAN AND CHAPTER OF YORK MINSTER

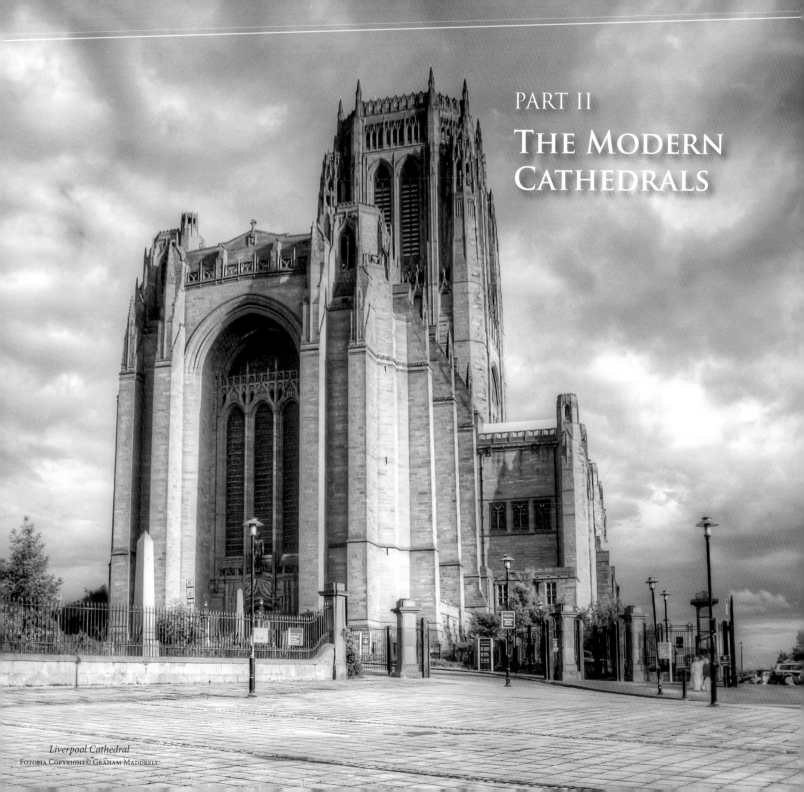

PART II
THE MODERN CATHEDRALS

Liverpool Cathedral
FOTOLIA COPYRIGHT © GRAHAM MADDRELL

COVENTRY

The new Diocese of Coventry, created in 1918, made its cathedral in the Parish Church of St. Michael. It was in every way a magnificent building. There had been a cathedral in Coventry before the Reformation, serving the Diocese of Lichfield and Coventry, and from time to time, each city would be named first. But St. Michael's cathedral was destroyed on the night of November 14th 1940 by German bombs, and only the tower and spire were left. The initial impulse to rebuild in the Gothic style was dropped in favour of an entirely twentieth century building which could speak of something beautiful and hopeful arising from the ashes of war.

Basil Spence's design won the competition with its gentle echoes of a nave-and-aisle scheme with a vault, but expressed by modern building methods, in concrete, and involving major contributions from some of the finest British artists of the day. In 1962 after only six years in the building, a cathedral at right angles to the old, faced with sandstone and green slate and with an entrance wall of engraved glass, opened its generous interior to an uninterrupted view of Graham Sutherland's vast Aubusson tapestry of Christ in Majesty.

Sir Jacob Epstein's expressionistic bronze of St. Michael overcoming the devil dominates the flight of entrance steps while the southern glass wall has a vast porch and a piazza enclosed by the ruined walls of the old Sanctuary.

Inside, on the east side, John Piper's great Baptistery Window still takes the breath away. Majestic organ pipes and choir stall "canopies" which rise like flights of birds, flank the High Altar and the tapestry.

It would be hard to think of any event more fitting to this great building than the deeply moving premiere of Benjamin Britten's War Requiem written for the cathedral's consecration in 1962, when the singing of Peter Pears and Dietrich Fischer Dieskau left not one dry eye. Britten used some of Wilfred Owen's poems and "Strange Meeting" was the final text:

"I am the enemy you killed, my friend.
I knew you in this dark; for so you frowned
Yesterday through me as you jabbed and killed.
I parried; but my hands were loath and cold.
Let us sleep now…"

www.coventrycathedral.org

A personal pilgrimage

'Reconciliation' by Josefina de Vasconcellos, 1995
FOTOLIA COPYRIGHT© MICHAL VALACH

GUILDFORD

The austerity of the monastic tradition and the poetry of light in monastic spaces is superbly caught by Sir Edward Maufe's brick-built cathedral on Stag Hill, designed in 1932 and completed by 1965 when the Queen attended the consecration. Guildford's parish church was too small to be the cathedral of the new diocese, made from a division of the Diocese of Winchester in 1927, so an architectural competition was held and eighty-three entries submitted. As in his extensions at Bradford Cathedral, Maufe's neo-Gothic is very pointedly pointed and in Guildford has a Cistercian purity, although some roof decoration is allowed.

In his own guide book, Maufe tells us that he wanted to produce a design based on the great English cathedrals and relying on proportion, mass, volume and line rather than on "elaboration and ornament". He succeeded. This unique building, which was paid for by the people and built of red bricks which they could buy and have inscribed with their initials for 2s6d each (!) is truly owned by the Christians of Guildford and its diocese. Some commentators have been scathing about the fittings in the cathedral but when we remember that the same impulse of the ordinary person lies behind them, we realise that Guildford Cathedral is not a holy art gallery, but a beacon of faith alive with the light of Understanding.

www.guildford-cathedral.org

A personal pilgrimage

Aerial view of Guildford Cathedral
PHOTO BY DAVID HOGG. REPRODUCED WITH PERMISSION OF GUILDFORD CATHEDRAL

Guildford Cathedral - long view towards baptisry
REPRODUCED WITH PERMISSION OF GUILDFORD CATHEDRAL

LIVERPOOL

The biggest cathedral in the world apart from St. Peter's in Rome, Liverpool Anglican Cathedral of Christ was the inspiration of the 22 year old Giles Gilbert Scott, son of Sir George. It is a supreme, breathtaking masterpiece inside and out, with a tower reaching to 331ft and needing an electric lift, and a total length of 619ft. The Lady Chapel alone has the majesty and size of a cathedral, and the nave, with its vast stone bridge and gallery, defies description. The cover for the font is a work of cyclopean proportions, as is the monument to the first President of the Cathedral Committee, the 16th Earl of Derby, of which even Death itself would be envious.

FOTOLIA COPYRIGHT© CARSON LIU

Work started in 1904 and in 1978 the service marking its completion was televised. The site was, and is, dramatic – a wooded quarry with lovely greens and paths on one side, and the waterfront of Liverpool's River Mersey on the other.

The Lady Chapel was the first part to be completed and is very French in feeling with many elaborate ribs, parapets, and soaring shafts, given further textural interest by the pointing between the dressed red sandstone blocks. This opulence was quietly dropped as the vast main church developed from the east, although the titanic east window and carved altar piece remain in the spirit of the Lady Chapel. Scott altered his designs over the years, and died in 1960, seeing all but the final bays of the nave.

A place for great occasions, it comes fully to life in one of Mahler's great choral symphonies, and its nave galleries can house many extra musicians. This, of all cathedrals, is the place to walk, to pause, to savour the way in which space and light have been enclosed and directed. In Liverpool Cathedral, the human spirit soars, and on taking its regretful leave, feels healed and transformed.

www.liverpoolcathedral.org.uk

A personal pilgrimage

TRURO

With its three matching towers and spires looking very Norman-French in style, Truro Cathedral comes as a dramatic surprise from the railway and dominates the lively city with a radiance rarely encountered in England. This was a conscious decision by its architect John Loughborough Pearson (1817-97), to create a church which looked as though it could be in Brittany, a region with light very similar to that of Cornwall.

The long fought-for Diocese of Truro was established in 1876, with Edward White Benson as its first bishop. He shared Pearson's vision and held out for a completely new cathedral for Cornwall instead of an enlarged parish church, although the south aisle of Truro's old St. Mary's church was incorporated into the new design.

Benson and Pearson wanted a cathedral of majestic and surprising vistas, unfolding as one walked around. This they achieved, and there is no screen blocking the vista from west to east, but some dramatic south-eastern arcades and changes of level as the old aisle of St. Mary's is entered. Pearson's son Frank carried on the work after his father's death, and having begun in 1880, the cathedral was finished in 1910, in the Early English style.

The West Front, refreshingly small, dominates the tiny square in front of it in a dramatic and very continental manner. Inside, the cathedral's great Willis organ has the power to wake the dead, and finer points of musical interpretation can become blurred, but this seems the only overwhelming component of this otherwise very impressive and friendly masterpiece.

www.trurocathedral.org.uk

A personal pilgrimage

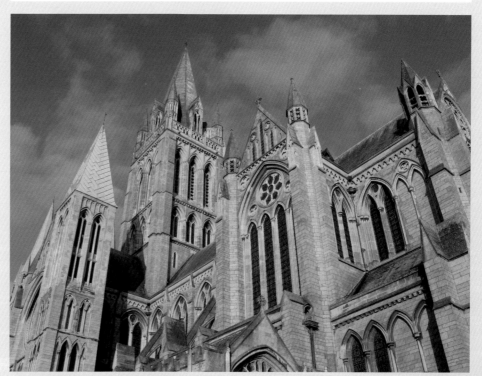

Truro Cathedral
FOTOLIA COPYRIGHT© MACH

PART III
THE PARISH CHURCH CATHEDRALS

Birmingham Cathedral
FOTOLIA COPYRIGHT© SUTTONBAGGIES

BIRMINGHAM

The new Diocese of Birmingham was created in 1905. Thomas Archer, architect of St. John's, Smith Square, London, built this Church of St. Philip in the early eighteenth century in the Baroque style with convex and concave elements in the tower and a splendid parapet. Four magnificent windows by Birmingham's own Sir Edward Burne-Jones and two superb eighteenth century organ cases bring distinction to the elegant interior.

www.birminghamcathedral.com

A personal pilgrimage

BLACKBURN

Consecrated in 1826 and becoming a cathedral exactly a century later, John Palmer's early Gothic Revival Church of St. Mary the Virgin has a number of modern additions which reflect its status, including a dramatic corona above the High Altar, by artist John Hayward. It is encrusted with large crystal jewels and hangs in the Lantern Tower in memory of the First Provost, John Sinker, and in gratitude for the preparations he made for the cathedral's extensions.

Palmer's nave has some superb roof bosses which should not be missed.

www.blackburncathedral.com

A personal pilgrimage

BRADFORD

The new diocese was created in 1919. Inside, the cathedral has great dignity, being essentially a fifteenth century church with many modern additions, including a chancel, ambulatory, three chapels and a chapter house designed by Sir Edward Maufe in the 1960s. Maufe's arcades are very pointedly pointed, and create a spacious Sanctuary. There are some William Morris windows in the Lady Chapel and a fine memorial by John Flaxman. Outside, a squat fifteenth century tower is flanked by wings built in the 1950s which hide the rest of the cathedral, but a modern cathedral close has been successfully designed around it all.

www.bradfordcathedral.co.uk

A personal pilgrimage

CHELMSFORD

The Parish Church of St. Mary the Virgin and St. Peter and St. Cedd became a cathedral in 1914. It is light, elegant and spacious. A magnificent fifteenth century tower remains from the ancient church. The nave collapsed in 1800, but was rebuilt with a superb roof by John Johnson. This rebuilding has itself undergone major internal restoration and reorganisation in the 1980s. In 1926, the chancel was extended, and in 1929 a chapter house and vestries were added. A superb new Chapter House was built in 1990. In 1994 a stunning new organ by N.P Mander Limited was installed beneath the west tower. Mark Cazalet's Tree of Life mural was recently fitted into the tracery of a blocked-up 20ft high window in the north transept. Other striking contemporary artworks adorn this radiant cathedral.

www.chelmsfordcathedral.org.uk

A personal pilgrimage

DERBY

Derby became a cathedral in 1927. Robert Bakewell's great wrought-iron gates, inside and outside, are highlights. Born in Uttoxeter in 1682, Bakewell died in 1752. The delicate gates simply divide, rather than screen off, the Sanctuary and Retrochoir, with the neo-classical Baldacchino or altar canopy, all designed by Sebastian Comper and completed in 1972. The superb tower (1530) of the original collegiate church remains, while the classical nave of 1723, is by the great James Gibbs. There are superb monuments by Rysbrack, Nollekens and Chantrey, and a much earlier one to the great Bess of Hardwick.

www.derbycathedral.org

A personal pilgrimage

LEICESTER

Leicester became a cathedral in 1927 and is the Parish Church of St. Martin. It is almost entirely Victorian and has charming grounds. The tower and spire of 1867 are by Raphael Brandon, superb, right angled buttressing giving way to twelve elegant lancets, then a broach spire with gabled lancets soaring to 220ft. The Lady Chapel is medieval and has fine eighteenth century furnishings, and there are fine memorials in the Herrick Chapel. The galleried entrance porch is rich in figure sculpture. Also involved in this cathedral were those great Gothic revival architects G.F. Street and J.L. Pearson.

www.cathedral.leicester.anglican.org

A personal pilgrimage

MANCHESTER

The Parish Church of St. Mary, St. George and St. Denys became Manchester Cathedral in 1847. It feels like an important place and was indeed built from 1422 as a collegiate parish church for a college of secular canons. It has some very fine woodwork, including a fifteenth century pulpitum, choir stalls, and nave roof. The fan vaulting beneath the tower is of the nineteenth century, because in 1867 the tower was partly rebuilt. The Victoria Porch at the foot of the tower commemorates Queen Victoria's Diamond Jubilee in 1897.

In 1970, a moving memorial service was held here for Sir John Barbirolli, one of the greatest conductors of all time and Conductor Laureate of Manchester's Hallé Orchestra which he rebuilt to world acclaim.

www.manchestercathedral.org

A personal pilgrimage

NEWCASTLE UPON TYNE

In 1882 the large Parish Church of St. Nicholas became a cathedral and unusually it did not need the extensions which have proved so necessary in the case of other parish church cathedrals. But it did receive, at that time, a new pulpit, screen and reredos.

The sixteenth century Maddison Memorial is one of the most beautiful in Britain. Beneath a broken pediment alive with figures and armorial shields, six kneeling figures pray inside scalloped niches while many more family members pray on a bas-relief plinth. Gilded Corinthian columns frame the exquisitely polychromed figures. There is also a seventeenth century organ case and a fourteenth century glass roundel with the Virgin and Child.

www.stnicholascathedral.co.uk

A personal pilgrimage

PORTSMOUTH

In October 1990 Diana, Princess of Wales, attended the completion of the final stage of this building, which became a cathedral in 1927. The new west front with its twin towers now makes a striking ensemble with the domed lantern on top of the plain Jacobean central tower. The twelfth and thirteenth century Sanctuary and Choir were augmented from 1927, with a new nave and aisle, which although doubling the size of the church, has left an uneasy architectural "stand-off" between the Gothic, and bold Classical columns and arches. In the "Navy Aisle" are many naval items of great interest, and overall, the feeling is akin to being inside a seventeenth century Dutch church interior as painted by De Witte or Saenredam.

www.portsmouthcathedral.org.uk

A personal pilgrimage

ST. EDMUNDSBURY

The great Benedictine Abbey of Bury St. Edmunds founded at the place to which the martyred Kind Edmund was brought in 903, now lies in a picturesque and superbly gardened ruin, while the Parish Church of St. James, which became the cathedral in 1913 (after having almost become one twice before) dominates with its Norman tower.

In the late twentieth century, Stephen Dykes Bower designed spacious extensions and more are planned. Flights of stone steps leading to dramatic vistas, a long, noble nave, and a feeling that one is moving around in a vast monastery, characterise this very atmospheric cathedral.

www.stedscathedral.co.uk

A personal pilgrimage

SHEFFIELD

Sir Charles Nicholson's extensions to Sheffield Cathedral were well underway, and would have included a new nave when the Second World War intervened. On the day before building was due to begin in September 1939, all normal life ceased. The comfortably proportioned Perpendicular Parish Church, with its magnificent Talbot monuments, became a cathedral in 1913 but had to wait until 1966 for its reconsecration, by which time an imposing detached south porch, and spacious descent into a dramatically enlarged west end with a lantern, had gone some way towards giving a much grander look to the ensemble. Some commentators feel uneasy about the marriage of old and new here, but walk in and walk around, and you will find two churches in one, as the west-east vista turns northwards into a raised chapel, and the eye continues beyond that.

Sheffield Cathedral offers an oasis of dramatic, calm spaces in the very heart of the bustling, cheerful city.

www.sheffieldcathedral.org

A personal pilgrimage

WAKEFIELD

A dramatic Perpendicular Parish Church with a soaring crocketted and pinnacled spire, Wakefield Church of All Saints became a cathedral in 1888 with Bishop Walsham Howe, whose memorial is within. Sir George Gilbert Scott, J.T. Micklethwaite and John Loughborough Pearson have all had a hand in this unusual building. Between 1897 and 1905 Pearson made further alterations and extended it sensitively in the Perpendicular style. The interior has a lavish feel – a rood designed by Sir Ninian Comper, good Victorian glass by Kempe, a fine organ case, superb roof bosses and much carved detailing in the woodwork lead to a gloriously vaulted Sanctuary and Retrochoir.

www.wakefieldcathedral.org.uk

A personal pilgrimage

Durham Cathedral,
cloister in Sunlight

GLOSSARY OF ARCHITECTURAL STYLES AND TERMS

All styles overlap

ROMANESQUE OR NORMAN

1066-1200. Characterised by round arches, huge solid walls and piers or columns, barrel or groin vaults, then simple ribbed vaults. Small window openings. Chevron or zigzag ornamentation.

EARLY ENGLISH

1175-1270. Pointed arches, thinner walls, columns with shafts and shaft rings, flying buttresses, tierceron or non-structural ribs, tall lancet pointed windows and geometrical and plate tracery based on circles with trefoil, quatrefoil or cinquefoil lobes inside the circles rather like pastry cuttings! The overall emphasis is on line, even to the ridge rib along the apex of the vault.

DECORATED

c.1250-1370. Elaborate curvilinear tracery and rib vaults, Ogee arches (S-shaped like flames), virtuoso carvings of leaves, animals and human forms. Rather more comfortable and softer version of the Early English.

PERPENDICULAR

c.1340-1550. Soaring shafts travelling straight up to vault ribs, lierne and fan vaults, slimmer columns and ribs, arches often less pointed. Interiors flooded with light from walls of glass, the windows having many panes.

ARCADE

A row of arches supported by columns.

BOSS

A carved stone disguising and beautifying the junction of several ribs.

CAPITAL

The carved stone 'cushion' at the top, or head, of a column.

CLERESTORY

A line of windows above the triforium or, as often in the Perpendicular period, directly above the main arcade.

CHOIR

The space beyond the Crossing to the east where the choir and clergy sit for services.

CROCKETTING

Carved projecting ornamentation on the side of a spire, pinnacle or gable.

CROSSING

The space where nave and main transepts intersect, normally carrying a central tower.

LIERNE RIBS

Ribs which travel star-shaped between the main vault ribs.

FAN VAULTS

A firework-like explosion of many ribs from a corbel or carved stone supporting a vault.

MANDORLA

The almond-shaped area in which the figure of Christ is often depicted.

MINSTER

From the Greek monasterion or monastery… The main or "mother" church of a geographic area. The word has nothing to do with size.

MISERICORDS

Wooden, hinged, forward-sloping seats in the Choir, which when tipped up reveal narrative carvings. These seats supported the clergy in long services.

NAVE

From the Latin for 'ship', the main body of the cathedral, often used for secular purposes, and with its vaulting often reminiscent of an upturned longship.

PRESBYTERY

The area to the east of the High Altar which normally contains many chapels.

PULPITUM

The screen which divides the nave from the choir.

SPANDREL

The wall space between arches, often left plain, but sometimes used for relief sculptures, or tracery.

TIERCERON RIB

A third rib in a vault, identical width but between two structural ribs.

TRANSEPT

One of the north-south arms of a cruciform-shaped church.

TRIFORIUM

An arcaded wall passage above the vault of the side aisle and above the aisle roof but beneath the clerestory.

TYMPANUM

The richly carved area above a doorway and bounded by an arch.

FURTHER READING

Anderson, William and Hicks, Clive: *Green Man*. Harper Collins 1990

Betjeman, John: *A Pictorial History of English Achitecture*. John Murray 1970

Clifton Taylor, Alec: *Cathedrals of England*. Thames and Hudson 1972

Cormack, Patrick: *English Cathedrals* (English Tourist Board). Weidenfeld and Nicholson 1984

Friar, Stephen: *The Sutton Companion to Cathedrals and Abbeys*. Sutton 2007

Johnson, Paul: *British Cathedrals*. Weidenfeld and Nicholson 1980

Owen, Dorothy (Ed.): *A History of Lincoln Minster*. Cambridge University Press 1994

Pevsner, Sir Nikolaus and Associates: *The Buildings of England*. Penguin 1964 (revised)

Raeburn, Michael (Ed.): *Sacheverell Sitwell's England*. Orbis 1986

Various authors: Romanesque – *Architecture, Painting, Sculpture*. Könemann 1997